Networking at
Writer's Conferences

Now available:

Networking at Writer's Conferences: From Contacts to Contracts, by
Steven D. Spratt and Lee G. Spratt

Book Editors Talk to Writers, by Judy Mandell

Networking at Writer's Conferences

From Contacts

to Contracts

STEVEN D. SPRATT
LEE G. SPRATT

John Wiley & Sons, Inc.
New York · Chichester · Brisbane · Toronto · Singapore

For Beck

This text is printed on acid-free paper.

This publication is designed to provide accurate and authoritative information in regard
to the subject matter covered. It is sold with the understanding that the publisher is not
engaged in rendering professional services. If legal, accounting, medical, psychological,
or any other expert assistance is required, the services of a competent professional
person should be sought.

Library of Congress Cataloging-in-Publication Data:

Spratt, Steven D., 1950–
    Networking at writer's conferences : from contacts to contracts /
  Steven D. Spratt, Lee G. Spratt.
        p.   cm.
    Includes bibliographical references.
    ISBN 0-471-05522-0 (pbk. : alk. paper)
    1. Authorship—Congresses.   2. Social networks.   I. Spratt, Lee
  G., 1950– .   II. Title.
  PN171.6.S67   1995
  808'.02—dc20   94-41639

10 9 8 7 6 5 4 3 2 1

Acknowledgments

THIS BOOK (and our career, for that matter) wouldn't have happened if we hadn't been blessed with the support and friendship of an assortment of people throughout the writing world. While we're probably forgetting at least a few, we'd like to thank Alta Mae Gaylord (thanks, Mom!); PJ Dempsey; Mary Alice Kier and Anna Cottle; Jean-Louis Brindamour and Ku, Fu-sheng; Mitch Douglas; Gerald (Jerry) Gross; Dr. Navnit Jayaram; Geri Jeter and KW Jeter, who give great parties and even better friendship; Michael Wm. Kasner; Hollis McMilan and the Markowitz, Herbold, Glade & Mehlhaf crew; Dr. Steven Mc-Clure; the Amazing Monica, without whom we can't see to write; Steve Perry; Dr. Edie Vickers; and our Monday night madhouse readers of *Illiterary Delusions* and brighteners of our lives. Thanks to one and all!

Contents

Introduction

IMAGINE WAKING UP one morning, rolling over to swat the alarm clock, and finding that your bed has been moved into the middle of a swirling crowd of hundreds of people who all seem to be speaking a foreign language and moving about with a purpose you can't quite fathom.

For most people, including us, that's what your first writer's conference is like.

You arrive confused, unsure of yourself, and amazed that you have managed to scrape together enough nerve to actually call yourself a writer in a room filled with *real* writers.

You feel like an impostor on the verge of being discovered.

You feel like an intruder.

You feel like the word "*ROOKIE*" is tattooed on your forehead in fluorescent green letters three inches high for everyone to see.

You finally realize, however, that these feelings come from within you, not from without. You start to relax. You work up the nerve to (*gasp*) ask a question, even though you're sure everyone will laugh at you. You compose yourself, take a deep breath, and in a trembling voice you cast forth your question—into an empty room.

You're too late; the conference is over.

So you gather up all the handouts you've collected over the course of the conference and slink out a side door, resolving that the next time—*the very next time*—all will be different. Next time, you'll be one of those lucky ones who made things happen, who made the contacts that turned into contracts. Who *networked*.

I.1 Why Are We Here?

Why, you might ask, are we talking about writer's conferences? Because, while you can network with other professionals in this business of writing at any time, anywhere, writer's conferences usually offer the best opportunity to network with the most professionals at one shot—*if* you do your homework and handle yourself properly. And that's what we're going to show you how to do. We can't do it for you (and wouldn't even if we could), but we can teach you how to do it for yourself. And the networking skills you'll learn will serve you in writer's conferences, at writer's group meetings, and on the occasional street corner—wherever you run into another writing professional.

Luck is where preparation meets opportunity, and that's what this book is all about. In these pages, we'll teach you how to effectively prepare for a writer's conference—whether it's your first time or your tenth. We'll teach you how to conduct yourself in such a way that you'll be treated like a professional even if it's your first conference and you've never sold a word. And we'll teach you how to come away from the conference with exactly what you came to get.

There's no magic to it, no mumbo jumbo, no difficult or abstract concepts. What you'll find in this book is a simple, direct, and *honest* way to network and use a conference to your best advantage.

If this sounds like a winner to you, put down your money and let's get on with it. If it doesn't, put this book back on the shelf where somebody who needs it can find it.

Time is money, and we've got work to do.

I.2 The Ins and Outs of Networking

Networking is perhaps the most prevalent, far-reaching, and powerful buzzword to come out of the late eighties and early nineties. It is the *process* behind the word that accounts for this book.

First, though, let's try to come up with a concrete definition of *networking*, a common basis of understanding we can all use to put the concepts and processes to work for us. Here's the Spratt definition: Networking is simply expanding the extent of your personal contacts and information by pooling your resources with others who have, or have access to, similar information.

For a writer, these sources of information can include other writers, agents, editors, booksellers, critics (expletives deleted)—people who are in the business of putting words on paper for the purpose of publication, people who transfer those published words into a form consumable by the reading public, and people who influence the sale of those words to the public.

The woods are full of 'em, and most have information that can be of use to you. But most also have some information that has worked for them (or maybe somebody they know), which could prove utterly useless, or even injurious, to your career.

How can you tell the difference?

I.3 Listen to It All; Use What Works for You

In our writing classes, we tell our students that they need to be receptive to all the information they come up with about writing and the business of writing that they can lay their ears or eyes on. We also tell them to take this information with a grain of salt. It's almost all valid for somebody, but it's not necessarily valid for you.

We include ourselves in the list of people from whom it is necessary to sort out the actually useful information—that information that pertains to how you go about doing what you do.

A good analogy for this process can be found in a gravel pit, believe it or not. Gravel must be sorted by size before it can be sold. It's fed into a shaker that has a series of screens with progressively smaller holes.

The first screen has large openings, so all but the largest gravel falls through onto the next screen. This largest gravel is then shunted off to the side and sold as is. This process is repeated through several screens until there's nothing left but sand.

You can use the same process in sorting information on the basis of usefulness. Just like you wouldn't use sand to build the base for a roadway, or fist-sized rocks to make mortar to put between bricks in a wall, some information is just not useful for what you're trying to do. It may not be useful for you at this time, or not applicable at all to you and your career. Learn how to run all the information you hear or read through your own personal screens of applicability.

We hear you out there: Okay, how do I tell what's applicable to me now and what's not?

Some of the information will conflict with your personality, with your concept of who you are, either personally or as a writer. It'll come across as something that you just wouldn't be comfortable doing, or as something in conflict with your belief systems. For example, we don't write for religious markets—spiritual markets maybe, but not church markets. It's just not us. But that doesn't mean it might not be a good choice for you.

There might be areas in which you have no expertise or no present interest in gaining expertise. Farm journals, sports magazines, and hard-core technical computer magazines among others (many others) fall into this category for us.

It might be a methodology that conflicts with your own sense of what's right and what's wrong, your sense of honor. We won't lie, cheat, or steal to make a sale. We won't use another person to make a sale. We won't abuse a friendship to make a sale. We won't do anything to make a sale that makes us feel ashamed or dirty for having done it. Life is too short, and what goes around always comes around.

What we will do, and have done for over a decade at the time of this writing, is realize that we are writers twenty-four hours a day, seven days a week, fifty-two weeks a year.

We realize that any conversation may contain the beginnings of a story idea, or plant the seed for a character, or put us onto information about a possible market, or help us find a new friend.

I.4 If You're Chasing a Dream, Hang Out with Dream Chasers

Friends. Where would we be without them? Our friends are, almost without exception, people who are actively pursuing an interest in the arts. Most of them are chasing one dream or another. Writers, of course, dominate the group. We understand writers best, and writers understand us best. We understand what makes them tick.

But our friends also include musicians, songwriters, glassworkers, poets, painters, sculptors, calligraphers, and others. We understand them, too.

And our friends also include publishers, editors, agents, and book-sellers. Just because these are primarily business contacts doesn't mean that they're any less our friends. On the contrary, in virtually all cases they are friends first and business contacts second.

We prefer to work our business within the framework of friendship whenever possible. It's easier on the stomach lining, for one thing. Business is more relaxed when both parties involved are on the same side of an issue, when both are pursuing the same goal.

So we talk often in this book about making friends and the different opportunities to make friends. Our method of networking is just that—making friends.

*We do not **use** our friends or our friendships* to make our business run. We only use the information our friends willingly and openly pass on to us. We use our contacts to open doors and to give our writing a fair and honest shot on the open market—if the contact is freely given.

We do not use our friends.

Our friends do not use us.

The nature of friendship, as we see it, is to help your friends wherever and whenever you can. We're not saying that you should give away your house, but if you have information that will help one of your friends, without taking food from your mouth in the process, that information should be freely given: not traded, not sold, but *given*.

And the delightful thing is, we've found that the world is filled with people who will give freely of their time and their knowledge, with no thought of recompense.

So, as you read through this book, you'll see that we refer to the process of networking as a process of making friends. It's as much a philosophy and a way of life as it is a way of getting your business of writing up and running.

The first fourteen chapters, and by far the largest portion of this book, teach you an effective, low-stress way to network at a writer's conference. Chapter 15 teaches you about some of the many other networking opportunities that abound in our writing world. We haven't even tried to list them all; that would be an exercise in futility. What we have done is to try to give you an overview—enough information that you will be able to spot networking opportunities when they pop up in front of you.

We didn't invent this method of networking. The fact is, it evolved for us. It evolved for a huge assortment of other writers who were once at the same stage of their careers as you are now.

I.5 Absolutely No Absolutes . . . Well, Almost

There's a habit common among speakers and teachers of writing that you will hopefully never see in these pages: if we ever tell you that you *have* to do something (aside from always enclosing a self-addressed, stamped envelope, of course), feel free to throw the book at us. Absolutes are (nearly always) nonsense in writing. Your job isn't to try to succeed using exactly the same methods as any another writer (not even us). Instead, read, listen, and learn everything you can; then sift through what you've heard, and use the bits and pieces that ring true for you. But don't throw away the parts that don't work for you right now. Somewhere down the line, you may well find out that you need some of those pieces.

I.6 Ideas to Work By

We repeat a number of themes or statements with some frequency. So that you're prepared when you run across them, here are a few of the major points you'll see:

- Good manners are good business.
- Say "thank you"—whatever the response.
- You'll learn more with your ears open and your mouth shut.
- Luck is where preparation meets opportunity.
- You make your own opportunities. No one else can make them—or use them—for you.

There—you should be ready to dive in. Enjoy the ride!

Part One

Before the Conference

1

What Is a Writer's Conference?

WRITER'S CONFERENCES and conventions come in all shapes and sizes. They may be one-day gatherings of ten or twenty people interested in a single aspect of writing, or multiday sessions of several hundred writers interested in everything from poetry to erotica. They may also be formal, often accredited, programs like the Iowa Writing Workshop and Clarion East/West, where writers spend large amounts of money and time getting what they're after. In every case, the goal of the writers attending the gathering is essentially the same: to learn how to write better, how to sell better, and how to walk up to a writer whose work you've admired your entire life and say, "Hi, I'm a writer, too"—without fainting. In other words, the goal is to improve your art, polish your craft, and learn how to network.

In every case, with every conference, networking opportunities abound. It's nearly impossible to attend a writer's conference *without* meeting people who could prove important to your writing career. The trick is to meet those important people as one professional (yes, we mean you) to another, whether or not you've ever sold a word.

1.1 Definitions

In order to ensure a shared level of understanding, let's review the meanings of primary job titles within the writing world and some other writing-related terms. (If you've been writing professionally for any length of time, skip this part, or skim through it as a refresher if you want to.)

1.1.1 Writer

Easy, right? Well, how often have you caught yourself responding with, "Oh, I'm not *really* a writer" when someone asks what you've published. There's a very simple, but absolutely essential, definition: *a writer is someone who writes*—in any genre, to any length, for any market. Remember that. In fact, it's not a bad idea to print out that definition in large, bold type and hang it somewhere so every time you sit down to write, you can't help but see it. If you're writing, you're a writer, regardless of where or what you've published—or even *if* you've published.

1.1.2 Editor

Many writers have a variety of seminasty definitions for this one, but since we've both edited and have good friends who are editors, we won't pass those on. Sarcasm aside, an editor is someone who revises (or suggests revisions of) written material the editor did not write. The editor is often also responsible for overseeing the entire project, whether book or magazine, from beginning to end. In most cases, editors work for *publishers*, who hold the purse strings and sometimes (but not always) own the *publishing house* or company that is doing the publishing. In certain fairly rare cases, the editor and publisher may be the same person.

An editor is also a creature with an extremely long memory, so it will serve you well to mind your manners when dealing with any editors for whom you are writing or wish to write. In fact, minding your manners when dealing with *all* editors (and other pros, too) is an extremely good idea. Many an editor will tell you that she doesn't remember bad writing—or, more precisely, the name of the writer who *performed* the bad writing—and that's in all probability the truth. However, rudeness, discourtesy, unprofessionalism, and bad manners *do* get remembered, and while we don't know of any writers who have actually been blacklisted (at least not since the days of Joe McCarthy), editors do talk to one another, and names are, on occasion, mentioned. *One of the fastest ways to become a professional writer is to begin using professional courtesy today.* Attitude and aptitude go hand in hand, and every editor knows this.

1.1.3 Literary Agent

A literary agent is a salesperson who works for a writer. Some agents may object strongly to this definition, but, to our way of thinking, that really is the core of the relationship. An agent serves the same purpose as a commissioned salesperson (or sometimes, marketing director), with the writer in the role of manufacturer.

While we recognize that the process of creating the written form involves art, when we're done, what we've produced is a product. It is the agent's job to know where, when, how, and to whom to sell that product to the writer's best advantage. Good agents do exist, and they're worth their weight in gold. For lists of agents, check industry directories such as the *Literary Market Place* or the *Guide to Literary Agents and Art/Photo Reps*, both listed in the Bibliography.

At present, most American literary agents charge a commission of 15 percent on domestic sales (with higher commissions usually applying to foreign sales). This generally means that of every dollar the agent earns for the writer, the agent receives fifteen cents. A few agents still charge just 10 percent domestic commission, but 15 percent has become pretty much the standard.

In addition to commissions, some agents also charge an initial reading fee, which can be anywhere from $35 to $500 (sometimes even higher). In other words, to be considered for representation by the agent, a new writer must pay a fee, which is usually nonrefundable. Paying this fee does not mean that the agent has agreed to represent you; the fee simply pays for the agent's consideration and feedback. While some people in our business will try to tell you that no reputable agent charges a reading fee, the reality is that this is no longer entirely true.

Many agents are in business for themselves or in a small partnership, and looking at unknown quantities (a writer with no track record) costs time and money. Often, a reputable agent will charge a nominal fee to recoup this time. It's up to you to figure out if the fee charged is worth the value received. (And you have every right to ask what you will get for your money: How many agents will look at the work? Will you receive a written critique? If so, how long will it be? How long will it take the agent to get back to you? Will you have a chance to revise and resubmit under the same fee?) If you feel the value is worth it, go for it; if it isn't, pass.

While the Raymond Carvers and Isaac Asimovs of the world may have had agents handling their short work, for the rest of us, agents almost exclusively handle book-length material (and, of course, film and other subsidiary rights). Most short fiction or nonfiction simply doesn't produce enough money to make it worth the agent's while. We have a pair of truly wonderful agents who handle all our book-length work, but we market all of our short fiction ourselves. Finding an agent who is willing to handle poetry is tantamount to locating a needle in a haystack. Agents have to make a living, and few poets can actually live on what they make, so how could an agent live on 15 percent of not-enough-to-live-on? (We'll go into substantially more detail on the selection, care, and feeding of agents in later chapters.)

1.1.4 Marketing

No, we're not talking groceries here. In this context, marketing is the art of identifying the publishing house, magazine, production company, or other agency that is most likely to purchase your writing, then submitting your writing in the manner most likely to encourage the purchase of your work. In addition, a vital (and often overlooked) part of the marketing process is identifying the best person to contact at that elusive purchaser, "best" being defined as "the person with both the inclination and the ability to say *yes*." We'll discuss both how to identify—and, more important, how to reach—that person in later chapters.

You should also understand some specific marketing terms, including *market* (who will pay you for your work), *audience* or *readership* (the person or age group ideally suited to read or hear your work), and *slant* (your selected market's usual attitude or angle on a given subject).

1.1.5 Schmoozing (Better Known as Networking)

Schmoozing is the art of making professional contacts that pay off (and, in its finest form, turning those contacts into friends). It's now better known as *networking*, and we'll be using the two terms interchangeably. It doesn't matter how shy you are (we're both *very* shy), where you live (even 'way out here in Portland-land-of-lumberjacks-Oregon), how you dress (we *live* in blue jeans and t-shirts), or any other barrier you can imagine. You, too, can learn to network, effectively and successfully, and you can turn your networking contacts into dollars. Virtually every chapter of this book contains references to, or pointers on, networking. Start practicing them as soon as you can, whether in the elevator in your office building, at the grocery store, or at your next writer's group meeting, and watch your confidence grow. We tend to think in terms of networking/schmoozing (and writing, for that matter) as being a muscle. If you don't use it, it atrophies; but use it regularly and consistently, and you can build the confidence necessary to schmooze at the snazziest cocktail party or with the snootiest editor.

1.1.6 The Work

When we refer to "the work" or "your work," we will be talking about a piece of your writing (whether in the form of manuscript, submission packet, or proposal) that is prepared in the proper format for consideration by a publisher or agent. (See 8.3 for more information on submission specifics.)

1.1.7 Self-Addressed, Stamped Envelope (SASE)

This envelope shows your name and address as the addressee. It should be of sufficient size to comfortably hold all the papers you expect to receive back, and have enough postage already attached to cover the mailing costs of those same pages. If you're not sure how much postage to use, take the package to your local post office and weigh it, with all the papers you wish to have returned. And don't forget, your outer envelope will need enough postage for all the papers *and* your return envelope. The SASE is a tool of vital importance to editors and agents, since it saves them the time and money necessary to mail your materials back to you. In fact, virtually any editor or agent in the business will not return materials without a SASE, so don't forget it.

1.1.8 Writing

If you're like most writers, you define writing by whatever type of written word you produce. Here are a few (very simplistic) definitions of types of writing (not intended in any way to be complete or exhaustive):

Fiction—Writing that is not true or did not actually happen, although it can be based on factual events and/or real people; it can be more true than fact in some cases. Types include *genre* (so-called categories, including mystery, western, science fiction), *mainstream* (difficult to define, but sometimes described as "fiction that doesn't fit into a genre"—helpful, isn't it?), and *literary* (even more difficult to define—"not genre, but off the beaten path" or "mainstream, but more complex" might work; for examples, read through the "little" or literary magazines). Common forms include the short story, novella, novelette, and novel.

Nonfiction—Writing that is based on factual information. It includes journalism, biography and autobiography, commentary, personal reminiscence, how to, self-improvement, and the like. Forms include articles, essays, and books.

Poetry—Writing that deals with imagery and form, rather than necessarily telling a story. Poetry can be either *rhyming* or *nonrhyming* (*prose poem*), *structured* or *unstructured*; can involve virtually any subject; and can appear in any of several dozen forms, from classical to modern.

Script—Writing intended to be performed, either on stage for a live audience, on radio, or for recording on either audio or videotape, or as a motion picture. It can be fiction or nonfiction, or even poetry (Shakespeare, anyone?).

Children's—Writing in any of the above types, but aiming for an audience usually younger than eighteen years old. It is frequently divided by age group of readership or length/type of published book (for example, sixteen- or thirty-two-page picture book, young adult, and so on).

1.2 But What Is a Writer's Conference, Really?

A large part of writing success is directly attributable to whom you know and how much you've learned. One of the best ways to get both "whos" and "whats" is to network your way through a writer's conference, where writers, editors, agents, and teachers gather to share their expertise and experience with other writers, or, as we describe it in our own career, to "pay forward."

Your reasons for going to a writer's conference may be to learn from these pros, absorb some of their know-how, and make your own business contacts. Or you may simply go for the pleasure of spending time with others who are following the same dream, and to unlearn three misconceptions shared by many new (and not so new) writers:

- You're crazy for wanting to write.
- It's impossible to make a living through your writing.
- Published writers, editors, and agents come from a different planet than unpublished writers.

No matter what the outside (nonwriting) world may tell you, this dream you're chasing *can* be caught, if you do your homework and learn everything you can before, during, and after the conference, and then apply what you've learned in every aspect of your writing life.

1.3 Why Should You Spend Your Time and Energy Doing Something That's Not Writing?

Sure, attending a writer's conference (and the research we'll have you performing before you go) will take time away from your writing. But what's the point spending all your time writing if you have no idea what happens next? By going to the right writer's conference for you and your writing, spending your time in carefully planned networking, and following up on your well-made contacts once you get home, you'll be giving yourself a leg-up on the rest of the competition. And, if all goes well, you will have laid the groundwork that will get your writing in front of the right people at the right time, thereby giving you more incentive to write (and hopefully more income to ease the stress of wondering how can you afford to write).

If you can be honest with yourself about your abilities and the areas in which you need improvement, and if you're willing to apply what we suggest, you'll have a terrific start on the next stage of your writing career—a stage that will be more successful, more rewarding, and more enjoyable than you've experienced in the past.

2

Why Are All These People Really Here?

IN ORDER TO lay the groundwork for your networking and get the most out of your writer's conference, you need to do your homework. A fitting place to start is with any conference's most important asset: *people*. Who are these people, and why are they here?

2.1 Beginning Writers

Writers who are just starting out, or who have been writing for a number of years with few or no publishing credits to date, have the most reasons for attending writer's conferences, and conferences have the most to offer them in return.

In the pursuit of publishing credits (and fame and glory), writers should leave no contact unturned, and a conference can be an opportunity to explore a wide variety of educational experiences. Following are just a few of the reasons that may motivate newcomers to attend.

2.1.1 To Learn More about the Art of Writing

By attending hands-on writing classes, you can learn more about the numerous aspects of this art of ours. While successful writing requires a working knowledge of the nuts-and-bolts of the craft, it also demands that you learn how to find your personal voice, how to express that voice on paper, and how to evoke the emotions you want your audience to feel. You can also learn by listening to more experienced writers as they discuss how they create a flow of words and how they deal with the give and take of emotions involved. You can even learn how to better deal with some of your own frustrations in writing by hearing how published writers deal with *theirs*—and believe us, the frustrations don't go away just because your name is in print. Hearing someone with a whole column of titles in *Books in Print* talk about the terrors of facing the "white bull" (Hemingway's term for a blank piece of paper) can give you some perspective on your own problems, as well as a great opening line when you walk up and introduce yourself to that same writer.

2.1.2 To Learn More about the Craft of Writing

By attending both hands-on and lecture sessions, you can learn how to hone your craft skills until every word says exactly what you want it to say, and not a word or image or emotion is wasted or missing. Question-and-answer periods can be enormously helpful when solving specific problems, and you can often make a great impression on a speaker you want to reach by asking the right question at the right time. (Make sure you study chapter 7, "Questions You Should Never Ask and Why.")

2.1.3 To Learn More about the Business of Writing

Nearly every writer, of whatever level of experience, can benefit from hearing up-to-date information on the business aspects of writing. Conferences often draw experts from other fields (including lawyers, accountants, and organization experts), since many of the business details in a writing career are similar to those in other small businesses. (Of course, some are specific to writing but require expert assistance.) We met an expert on freelance tax issues for writers at a conference a number of years ago, and it gave us a great opportunity to verify answers on several general tax issues relating to our writing career. Copyright law, tax benefits, contracts, plagiarism, libel—all of these (and many more) business details are of vital importance to your career.

2.1.4 To Make New Contacts in the Business

We meet a lot of new writers who feel defeated before they've begun, because they think success is a matter of "It's not how or what you write, but who you know." Believe it or not, to a large extent, they're right. But don't feel discouraged by this fact, because you're forgetting the most important addendum: *No one is born knowing the "right people."* Every writer who has important and valuable contacts went out and made those contacts. Writer's conferences are a great place to begin making these new contacts, *if* (and this is an enormous "if") you handle yourself with professionalism and courtesy. It's what networking is all about.

2.1.5 To Renew Old Contacts in the Business

Once you've started making business contacts, you'll need to cultivate and maintain them. Use your writer's conference to renew any contacts you've made in the past, bringing them up-to-date on the progress of your writing and publishing and learning what they've been up to since you saw them last. Maybe that editor you impressed (but couldn't sell to) last year has changed jobs, and now needs *exactly* what you've spent the last year writing. Never consider any professional networking contact wasted; we've had them pay off four or five years after the initial meeting, in ways we'd never foreseen.

2.1.6 To Meet Old Friends and Make New Friends

Don't be afraid to view at least part of the conference as a chance to visit with old and new friends and acquaintances. Why? Because writers share experiences, frustrations, and attitudes. In addition, whenever possible, turn the business contacts you like into at least warm acquaintances. Why spend time working with someone you don't like? As an agent once told us, the writing world has more than its share of LITS writers ("Life Is Too Short" to deal with this person). This applies to writer's conferences, too.

2.1.7 To Find Out You're Neither Stupid Nor Crazy for Pursuing a Career in Writing

Writing is an extremely demanding taskmaster, as well as one of the few business situations where the default answer to any (and every) question is "no." Every published writer we know—ourselves included—has dealt with family members and friends who have pushed hard (sometimes very hard) on the writer in question (or worse, on the writer's spouse) to go out and get a "real" job. If you have a day job and can make time to write as well, you're one of the lucky ones. The rest of us battle to make ends meet and satisfy the Muse. We're never quite certain from one day to the next whether we've succeeded at either one. Just remember, *all published writers started out where you are now,* and they made it, which means you can, too.

2.2 Seasoned (Published) Writers

Why would an experienced writer, presumably with at least some publishing credits, spend time and money to attend a writer's conference?

No matter how long you've been writing, no matter how well you market, there are *always* more tricks to be learned and more networking contacts to be made. In addition, seasoned writers are frequently invited to speak or teach at conferences, allowing them to attend for free (or possibly even be paid), and giving them the opportunity to pay forward for help they received when they were getting started.

2.3 Literary Agents

By speaking at conferences (and, in many cases, providing free or paid consultations; see chapter 12 for more information), agents can make personal contacts with new and established writers and invite only those writers with whom they would consider working to submit manuscripts or queries.

Ideally, this saves everyone time and money: The writer is saved the expense, time, and frustration of submitting to an agent who isn't right for the writer or the work, and the agent is spared the time and aggravation of sorting through dozens (or sometimes hundreds) of unacceptable or inappropriate submissions. Of course, this method isn't foolproof (is anything?), but when it works, it encourages mutual respect and professionalism on both sides, and also—and most important—encourages agents to keep their doors open to new or beginning writers as possible clients.

You can network with agents just as you can with editors and other writers. Even if you're not yet ready to hook up with an agent, or you already have an agent you're happy with, making networking contacts with agents can sometimes lead to introductions to editors and writers you've been wanting to meet.

Attending conferences also gives agents an opportunity to meet socially with editors and publishers they might have only seen professionally in the past, thereby encouraging better relations, more sales, and even friendships. (See, even agents need to network!)

2.4 Editors

Why would an editor speak at a writer's conference? Simple. Every time an editor educates *just one* new writer on proper etiquette and submission technique, that's one writer who will be less likely to make some fatal error in the near future. Every time an editor tells a "bumbling amateur horror story" to an attentive crowd of new writers, at least some of those neophytes will learn from the experience, and won't make that same mistake in their careers. For every new writer who follows the rules, there's one more editor who will at least consider taking a flyer with a beginner.

Why do editors usually prefer to work with and buy from established writers? Here's the truth of the matter: Even though experienced writers may cost more in advances, they are almost always less expensive to work with. Experienced writers require less time and energy to edit as well as less explanation of requested revisions. So how do you, as a new or less established writer, sell your work? By behaving as a professional; showing respect for yourself, your work, and the editor; and recognizing which battles to fight and which battles to pass up. As Professor Hill taught in *The Music Man*, it's the "think system": *Think* like a professional, so that you *act* like a professional, and you will *become* a professional.

You might ask, "What can it matter if I mess up with one editor? There are always others." Well, editors talk to each other, and the writing world isn't really that big. Show some respect and behave professionally and, even if you do make a mistake, you'll probably be given a second (or third, or fourth) chance.

2.5 Writing Teachers

Outside the academic sphere, nearly every teacher of writing is also a writer. How this relates to your life and career depends on the teachers you deal with. Since the majority of writing teachers also write (and, hopefully, with some success), those same teachers will often have more practical, useful information and contacts to pass along to their students.

Be extremely careful when it comes to deciding which writing teacher(s) to learn from, particularly in writing classes outside a conference setting. In the first adult writing class we attended (through a local community school program), the teacher claimed she was published, but refused to give the title of the book, the pseudonym she used, or the publisher; she insisted on speaking in absolutes regarding truly personal choices such as style, outlining, endings, and so on; and she flatly refused to consider any views that conflicted with her own. Needless to say, we didn't stay long, and that experience is the main reason that our students are always given explicit permission to stop us any time we use an absolute—*except* where SASEs are concerned.

However useful and helpful good writing teachers can be, no teacher can create your style or write in your voice, and they shouldn't even try. Their job is to help *you* make the most of *your* voice and style. Remember to run what you learn from a writing teacher through the same sieve you use on every other piece of writing information you hear, including what you get from us. Listen to all of it, sort through it and find the nuggets that ring true for you and your writing, use what you can, and don't apply what doesn't fit.

2.6 General Observations about Speakers

To some extent, the speakers you'll meet at writer's conferences are people who happen to be farther along their career track than the writers attending the conference. Remember that they're still just people, susceptible to good and bad moods, exhaustion, irritation, and euphoria just like you are. They have many of the same doubts and fears you have. Remember, too, that they're attending the writer's conference to do business, just like you are. The more you recognize their humanity, the closer you are to being on equal footing with them, which puts friendship just around the corner.

3

Evaluating Your Status
as a Writer

A Questionnaire

BEFORE YOU CAN DECIDE which writer's conference, and which conference events, will give you the best value and provide you with the best networking opportunities, you need to have a firm idea of where you and your writing stand in the overall scheme of things. While there are as many variables as there are writers, we've narrowed the possibilities to a workable list of the major contenders. This is by no means a scientific testing method, but one based on our experience.

Good writing is good writing, whether you write fiction, nonfiction, or whatever. Characterization, plot, action, research, and the like are much the same in any form of writing. The tools you need to write great short stories are basically the same as those you need to write great articles, so look at each question as it applies to your work.

Base your art and craft answers on an objective appraisal of your three most recent articles, short stories, or chapters. (And if you can't be objective about your own writing, ask a writer who knows your work best and whom you respect most to help with the questionnaire.) For poetry, answer the questions that apply and ignore the areas that don't. In your answers to each question, be consistent in how you gauge your responses: "always" should be a 10, "most of the time" a 7 or 8, "hardly ever" a 2 or 3, "never" a 0, and so on.

In completing the following questionnaire, keep in mind two absolutely vital points: (1) no one else is going to see your answers (unless, of course, you ask another writer for help); and (2) *be honest*. If you're not honest with yourself about your abilities and weaknesses now, how are you ever going to deal with the writing world on an honest basis?

3.1 Art and Craft

3.1.1 Characterization

1. Are your primary characters or subjects strong enough (and/or intriguing enough) to carry the reader's interest?

   No   Yes
   0 1 2 3 4 5 6 7 8 9 10

2. Are your characters/subjects believable within the circumstances in which you've placed (or found) them?

   No   Yes
   0 1 2 3 4 5 6 7 8 9 10

3. Do your major characters/subjects have enough flaws to make them human (whether or not they are)? (Nobody wants to read about a saint unless your subject really was one.)

   No   Yes
   0 1 2 3 4 5 6 7 8 9 10

4. Does your work contain primary, secondary, and tertiary characters?

   No   Yes
   0 1 2 3 4 5 6 7 8 9 10

5. If your work is focused on a single character or subject, have you included enough detail and description to hold the readers' attention?

   No   Yes
   0 1 2 3 4 5 6 7 8 9 10

6. Do your characters/subjects act from believable motivations, based on their personalities and circumstances?

   No   Yes
   0 1 2 3 4 5 6 7 8 9 10

7. Can you identify your primary characters'/subjects' motivations?

No   Yes
0 1 2 3 4 5 6 7 8 9 10

8. Can your reader identify your primary characters'/subjects' motivations?

No   Yes
0 1 2 3 4 5 6 7 8 9 10

9. Do your characters/subjects behave consistently (or with consistent inconsistency) within their personalities and circumstances?

No   Yes
0 1 2 3 4 5 6 7 8 9 10

10. If your characters/subjects don't behave consistently, do you give sufficient evidence to support why they don't?

No   Yes
0 1 2 3 4 5 6 7 8 9 10

11. Do you include sufficient details about your major characters/subjects so your readers feel they know them?

No   Yes
0 1 2 3 4 5 6 7 8 9 10

12. Are the relationships among your characters/subjects believable?

No   Yes
0 1 2 3 4 5 6 7 8 9 10

13. Are the relationships between your characters/subjects and their circumstances believable?

No   Yes
0 1 2 3 4 5 6 7 8 9 10

3.1.2 Plot

1. Is your plot or the progression of your article factually accurate (no matter how fantastic the circumstances)?

No   Yes
0 1 2 3 4 5 6 7 8 9 10

2. Do your plot/progression points follow a logical flow?

No   Yes
0 1 2 3 4 5 6 7 8 9 10

3. Does your plot or progression flow naturally from your characters' or subjects' motivations, personalities, and circumstances?

No   Yes
0 1 2 3 4 5 6 7 8 9 10

4. Does your plot contain enough conflict to carry the story or article?

No   Yes
0 1 2 3 4 5 6 7 8 9 10

5. Can you identify the central conflict in your story in one sentence? (*high concept*)

No   Yes
0 1 2 3 4 5 6 7 8 9 10

6. Does your plot contain minor details that have a significance that becomes clear to the reader at a later point in the story? (*circles*)

No   Yes
0 1 2 3 4 5 6 7 8 9 10

7. Do all your circles close (for example, if you start any circles early in the story line, does the significance of the majority of them become clear by the end)?

No   Yes
0 1 2 3 4 5 6 7 8 9 10

8. If your story involves a mystery of some sort, are your false clues (*red herrings*) close enough to the real clues to create suspense?

No   Yes
0 1 2 3 4 5 6 7 8 9 10

9. Whatever the genre or form, does your story contain enough sense of expectation (*suspense*) to carry the reader through the story?

No   Yes
0 1 2 3 4 5 6 7 8 9 10

3.1.3 Action

1. Is there sufficient movement (whether physical or emotional) in your story or article to keep your readers involved?

   No   Yes
   0 1 2 3 4 5 6 7 8 9 10

2. Does the action in your story or article flow naturally from the characters' or subjects' motivations and personalities and the situations in which they find themselves?

   No   Yes
   0 1 2 3 4 5 6 7 8 9 10

3. Does the action in your story or article work smoothly within the plot or circumstances?

   No   Yes
   0 1 2 3 4 5 6 7 8 9 10

3.1.4 Beginnings

1. Does your story grab the reader's attention within the first three sentences? (*hook*)

   No   Yes
   0 1 2 3 4 5 6 7 8 9 10

2. Does your article begin with a sentence or paragraph that sets the tone and grabs the reader's attention? (*lead*)

   No   Yes
   0 1 2 3 4 5 6 7 8 9 10

3. Does your story/article move smoothly from the hook or lead into the main body of the story? (*transition*)

   No   Yes
   0 1 2 3 4 5 6 7 8 9 10

4. Does your story or article begin with one of your primary characters?

   No   Yes
   0 1 2 3 4 5 6 7 8 9 10

5. Does the beginning of your story or article set up a conflict involving one or more of your primary characters/subjects?

    No   Yes
    0 1 2 3 4 5 6 7 8 9 10

6. Does your lead set up an expectation (whether of information, solution of conflict, answers to questions, and so on) that draws the reader into the article?

    No   Yes
    0 1 2 3 4 5 6 7 8 9 10

3.1.5 Middles

1. Does the middle of your story or article tie the beginning and ending together?

    No   Yes
    0 1 2 3 4 5 6 7 8 9 10

2. Does the middle of your story or article give the reader enough information to give the ending logical weight?

    No   Yes
    0 1 2 3 4 5 6 7 8 9 10

3. Does the middle of your story or article contain sufficient plot details to support your conclusion?

    No   Yes
    0 1 2 3 4 5 6 7 8 9 10

3.1.6 Endings

1. Does your story end naturally (without "and then she woke up" or "it was all a dream" endings)?

    No   Yes
    0 1 2 3 4 5 6 7 8 9 10

2. Does your article ending tie up the threads you've scattered throughout the piece?

    No   Yes
    0 1 2 3 4 5 6 7 8 9 10

3. Is the ending of your story or article satisfying to the reader?

    No   Yes
    0 1 2 3 4 5 6 7 8 9 10

4. Does your ending satisfy *you?*   No   Yes
                                      0 1 2 3 4 5 6 7 8 9 10

5. Does your ending play fair   No   Yes
   (it doesn't rely on informa-   0 1 2 3 4 5 6 7 8 9 10
   tion known to the writer
   but withheld from the
   reader)?

6. By the end of your story or ar-   No   Yes
   ticle, has the primary con-   0 1 2 3 4 5 6 7 8 9 10
   flict you set up at the
   beginning been resolved?

3.1.7   Rhythm, Pacing, and Word Choices

1. Does the rhythm of your story   No   Yes
   or article fit its tone?   0 1 2 3 4 5 6 7 8 9 10

2. Is the pacing of the events in   No   Yes
   your story/article suitable to   0 1 2 3 4 5 6 7 8 9 10
   the subject matter and
   style?

3. Do your word choices fit your   No   Yes
   characters/subjects?   0 1 2 3 4 5 6 7 8 9 10

4. Are your narrative word   No   Yes
   choices appropriate for the   0 1 2 3 4 5 6 7 8 9 10
   age group, education level,
   and background of the audience you're writing for?

3.1.8   Dialogue

1. Do your characters or subjects   No   Yes
   have separate, clearly iden-   0 1 2 3 4 5 6 7 8 9 10
   tifiable voices (can your
   reader usually tell who's
   speaking without an attri-
   bution)?

2. Do your characters or subjects speak believably for their background and personality?

No   Yes
0 1 2 3 4 5 6 7 8 9 10

3. Do you inform your reader about outside details (surroundings, description, reaction) through dialogue?

No   Yes
0 1 2 3 4 5 6 7 8 9 10

4. Do you verify all quotes used in your articles?

No   Yes
0 1 2 3 4 5 6 7 8 9 10

3.1.9 Research

1. Do you perform subject matter research to support your work?

No   Yes
0 1 2 3 4 5 6 7 8 9 10

2. Do you flesh out information you've gained from interview sources with additional data from your own research?

No   Yes
0 1 2 3 4 5 6 7 8 9 10

3. Do you maintain research files on information you've gathered, in case you need to verify some fact later?

No   Yes
0 1 2 3 4 5 6 7 8 9 10

4. Do you cross-reference your notes for later access?

No   Yes
0 1 2 3 4 5 6 7 8 9 10

3.1.10 Faith, Perseverance, and Thoroughness

1. Do you most often feel good about a piece after you've finished it?

No   Yes
0 1 2 3 4 5 6 7 8 9 10

2. In your opinion, is the majority of your work usually fairly good, at least after you've revised it?

No   Yes
0 1 2 3 4 5 6 7 8 9 10

3. Do you finish the majority of pieces you start?

No   Yes
0 1 2 3 4 5 6 7 8 9 10

4. Do you feel optimistic about your future as a writer, at least most of the time?

No   Yes
0 1 2 3 4 5 6 7 8 9 10

5. Do you reread and revise every piece of your writing at least once?

No   Yes
0 1 2 3 4 5 6 7 8 9 10

6. Do you carefully proofread every piece of your work before you send it out for submission?

No   Yes
0 1 2 3 4 5 6 7 8 9 10

7. Do you allow a piece of your work to sit overnight between final revision and sending it out for submission?

No   Yes
0 1 2 3 4 5 6 7 8 9 10

3.2 The Business of Writing

3.2.1 Marketing

1. Have you studied the markets available for your type of writing?

No   Yes
0 1 2 3 4 5 6 7 8 9 10

2. Do you read writing magazines and other sources of market listings to keep your sales knowledge current?

No   Yes
0 1 2 3 4 5 6 7 8 9 10

3. Have you requested guidelines from at least three new markets in the past month?

No   Yes
0 1 2 3 4 5 6 7 8 9 10

3.2.2 Contacts

1. Do you attend writer's group meetings in order to make new contacts?

No   Yes
0 1 2 3 4 5 6 7 8 9 10

2. Do you know at least five writers in your field of interest who live in your hometown?

No · · · · · · · · · · · Yes
0 1 2 3 4 5 6 7 8 9 10

3. Do you know at least five *other* writers in completely unrelated fields of interest who live in your hometown?

No · · · · · · · · · · · Yes
0 1 2 3 4 5 6 7 8 9 10

4. If you attend a reading by an author you admire, do you make a point of introducing yourself and making a *personal* contact?

No · · · · · · · · · · · Yes
0 1 2 3 4 5 6 7 8 9 10

5. Do you keep track of and follow up on the personal business contacts you make?

No · · · · · · · · · · · Yes
0 1 2 3 4 5 6 7 8 9 10

3.2.3 Manuscript Mechanics

1. Do you know and consistently follow the format requirements for all the types of writing that you do?

No · · · · · · · · · · · Yes
0 1 2 3 4 5 6 7 8 9 10

2. Is every manuscript you send out the door on clean, unstapled white paper, printed with black ink, double-spaced, with one-inch margins, and with clearly numbered pages?

No · · · · · · · · · · · Yes
0 1 2 3 4 5 6 7 8 9 10

3. Does the first page of every manuscript you send out include your name, address, phone number, social security number, and estimated word count?

No · · · · · · · · · · · Yes
0 1 2 3 4 5 6 7 8 9 10

3.2.4 Categorizing Your Writing

1. Can you answer the question "What do you write?" in one or two brief sentences?

No   Yes
0 1 2 3 4 5 6 7 8 9 10

2. If someone asks about your current project, can you describe it in one sentence? (*high concept*, again)

No   Yes
0 1 2 3 4 5 6 7 8 9 10

3.2.5 Persistence

1. Do you send a *polite* follow-up letter if you haven't received a response to a manuscript or query? (*Note:* It's usually a good idea to give any editor at least one month extra, above and beyond the full response time stated in the guidelines or market listing.)

No   Yes
0 1 2 3 4 5 6 7 8 9 10

2. When you receive a rejection of a manuscript or query, how long does it take you to get back to writing? (If less than one day, give yourself a 10; if two days to one week, give yourself a 5; if over one week, give yourself a 0.)

No   Yes
0 1 2 3 4 5 6 7 8 9 10

3. Do you submit a rejected manuscript or reslant a rejected query to a new market within twenty-four hours?

No   Yes
0 1 2 3 4 5 6 7 8 9 10

3.2.6 Recordkeeping

1. Do you keep records of submissions of your work so
   that you always know exactly where each piece of
   writing or query is?

   No   Yes
   0 1 2 3 4 5 6 7 8 9 10

2. Do you keep track of your income and expenses for tax
   purposes?

   No   Yes
   0 1 2 3 4 5 6 7 8 9 10

3. If you write at home, do you
   take a home office deduc-
   tion on your tax return (if
   you qualify)?

   No   Yes
   0 1 2 3 4 5 6 7 8 9 10

3.2.7 What You Write

Mark *all* that apply:

FICTION

Forms

- **Short short stories** (according to *Novel & Short Story Writer's Market*, under 700 words)
- **Short stories**
- **Novellas/novelettes** (according to the same source, usually 7,000–15,000 words
- **Novels**

Types

- **Mainstream** (frequently defined as "anything that doesn't fit in a genre")
  - Contemporary
  - Men's
  - Women's
- **Genres** (from *Novel & Short Story Writer's Market*)
  - Adventure
  - Erotica
  - Children's/Juvenile

- Ethnic/Multicultural
- Experimental
- Family Saga
- Fantasy
- Feminist
- Gay/Lesbian/Bisexual
- Historical
- Horror
- Humor/Satire
- Literary
- Military/War
- Mystery/Suspense
- New Age/Mystic
- Psychic/Occult
- Regional
- Religious/Inspirational
- Romance
- Science Fiction
- Senior Citizen/Retirement
- Sports
- Thriller/Espionage
- Western
- Young Adult/Teen
- Other _____

NONFICTION

Forms

- Articles
- Books
- Sales/Advertising

Types/Subjects (obtained from *Writer's Market*)

- Advertising/Marketing
- Animal
- Architecture
- Art/Design
- Astrology/Metaphysics

- Automotive/Motorcycle
- Aviation/Space
- Biography
- Business/Finance
- Career
- Child Care/Parenting
- Children
- Collectibles
- Commentary
- Communications
- Consumer Services
- Detective/True Crime
- Disabilities
- Education
- Electronics
- Engineering
- Entertainment
- Ethnic/Minority
- Farming
- Fashion
- Food/Drink
- Games/Puzzles
- Gay/Lesbian/Bisexual
- Health/Fitness
- History
- Hobby/Craft
- Home/Garden
- How-To
- Humor
- Insurance
- Journalism
- Juvenile
- Law
- Lifestyles
- Literary
- Management
- Medicine
- Men's

- o Military
- o Music
- o Nature/Conservation
- o Opinion/Editorial
- o Personal Computers
- o Pets
- o Philosophy
- o Photography
- o Politics/World Affairs
- o Psychology
- o Real Estate
- o Regional
- o Relationships
- o Religious
- o Retirement
- o Rural
- o Science
- o Self-Improvement
- o Sports
- o Transportation
- o Travel/Camping/Trailer
- o Women's
- o Young Adult/Teen
- o Other _____

POETRY

Forms (from *Poet's Market*)

- o Beat
- o Epic
- o Haiku
- o Prose
- o Senryu
- o Tanka
- o Visual
- o Concrete
- o Experimental

- ○ Traditional
- ○ Other _____

Subjects

- ○ Children's
- ○ Ecology
- ○ Erotica
- ○ Ethnic
- ○ Fantasy
- ○ Feminism
- ○ Gay/Lesbian/Bisexual
- ○ Horror
- ○ Humor
- ○ Inspirational
- ○ Love/Romance
- ○ Nature
- ○ Political
- ○ Psychic/Occult
- ○ Regional
- ○ Religious
- ○ Rural
- ○ Science Fiction
- ○ Senior Citizen
- ○ Social Issues
- ○ Sports
- ○ Teen/Young Adult
- ○ Other _____

SCRIPTS

Forms

- ○ Industrial/Educational
- ○ Radio
- ○ Screenplay
- ○ Stage Play
- ○ Teleplay

Types

- ○ Thirty-/sixty-minute (Radio)

o Commercial (Radio)
o Short Subject (Film)
o Full-Length (Film)
o One-Act (Stage)
o Two-/Three-Act (Stage)
o Musical (Stage)
o Thirty-Minute Sit-Com (TV)
o Sixty-Minute Drama (TV)
o Movie-of-the-Week (TV)
o Miniseries (TV)
o Commercial (TV)
o Sales Video/Audio
o Other _____

3.3 Scoring the Questionnaire

After you've completed the questionnaire, let it sit overnight, or better yet, for a day or two. Then, go back over your responses one by one, review them carefully and change any you feel differently about.

Once that's done, break down the first two sections ("Art and Craft" and "The Business of Writing") into their separate parts by subheading. Add the numbers of your answers in each subcategory, then divide them by the number of questions in that subheading, to arrive at your average for that subcategory. For instance, suppose that in "Characterization" your responses are 6, 2, 3, 4, 0, 8, 7, 4, 4, 5, 0, 3, and 6. Add those together, for a total of 52. Divide that total by thirteen questions, and you have an average answer of 4. In other words, if these were your responses, you'd discover that, while you have some knowledge in the area, characterization probably isn't one of your strongest points. The writer's conference you choose to attend should include that subject as one of the major areas that will be covered.

Figure your average in each of the subcategories, and create a list of your averages, together with the types and forms of writing that catch your interest.

3.4   Please, No Hate Mail

This questionnaire is by no means foolproof. It is intended to be used only as a guide to help you decide which conference will do you the most good. You should remember that your answers will change over time. You should reanswer the questions for the next conference you plan to attend, if the timespan between them is over two months. If you attended any conference in between, you should have learned enough to change at least some of your answers. Also remember that we're not attempting in any way to disparage you or your writing, so please don't send us any hate mail saying we've scarred you for life because your plotting average was 3.

3.5   When in Doubt, Look It Up

As you go back through the questionnaire, jot down any terms we've used that you aren't familiar with. After you've worked the averages for the subcategories, turn to your copy of whatever primary market listing you're using (see the Bibliography for suggestions), and see if you can find definitions of those terms. If there are some terms you still can't figure out, call the writer with whom you feel the best connection, and see if you can work up definitions between you. If you're still stumped, call the office of the largest local writer's group and ask for their help. Your local library may also have a telephone reference line that could help for the more general terms, but they're not likely to be much help on industry-specific terms (the same holds true for an ordinary dictionary).

The point of this part of the exercise is to give you a basic understanding of the terminology of the writing trade. We've given you our definitions of many of the terms we thought might trip you up, but we've probably missed some.

4

Which Conference Is Right for You?

ONCE YOU'VE COMPLETED the questionnaire in chapter 3 to determine where you and your writing fit in the general scheme of things, how do you use this information to find the *right* writer's conference?

4.1 Narrow the Available Choices

Go through the conference listings you've gathered (see list at page 151, or check the May issue of *Writer's Digest*; there are also conference ads in most issues of *Writer's Digest* or *The Writer*) and pick out the conferences that fit your general requirements. Points to consider include the following.

4.1.1 Cost

Here's where reality rears its ugly head. Unless you happen to be independently wealthy, money is going to have a sizable influence on which conference you attend. Sit down and figure out what you can reasonably afford, without starving or stressing out, for your total conference outlay, including registration fee, travel, lodging, meals, and incidental expenses (and figure in a *small* amount for buying speakers coffee; see 10.9 for more about this). Don't let a small budget shut you out. While longer conferences or college-accredited programs are likely to be very expensive, weekend conferences quite often have registration fees in the neighborhood of $200 to $300. (And some, like most of the science fiction, fantasy, and horror conventions [Ory-Con, BayCon, WesterCon] may cost no more than $50!) Selecting a conference within commuting distance, or one on a college campus with available student housing, can also help keep your overall expenses to a minimum.

Another option you should consider (and one we'll be pushing in 10.1) is to volunteer to work on the conference. This can reduce your registration fee (frequently by as much as half), and give you a great chance to network in the process. Some conferences offer scholarships or time-payment plans, so don't be afraid to ask. In many cases, you'll have to join the sponsoring organization in order to volunteer or get a scholarship, but even with the membership fee, you can quite often save a substantial amount of money.

If you're interested in either volunteering or obtaining a scholarship, *ask early*. It's a good idea to ask about volunteering when you write or call for the conference brochure. If you miss this opportunity, call the conference information line *now* and ask to speak to the volunteer coordinator. Conference staffs always need more help, and there may be some jobs available even at the last minute. By volunteering early, however, you can usually have your pick of the available jobs. (See 10.1 for the best jobs to pick and why.)

4.1.2 Timing and the Length of the Conference

If you're working a day job, are the primary caretaker for young, disabled, or elderly family members, or have other family, social, or professional commitments to take into consideration, you'll need to determine how long a conference you can reasonably afford to attend. Remember to figure in travel time to and from the conference site, and how much lead time you'll need to either get vacation time from work or arrange alternate coverage for your responsibilities.

One especially helpful suggestion is to plan your time off, whether from a day job or other commitments, to allow yourself one free day after the conference. You're going to be exhausted, both physically and mentally, and you'll have work to do to follow up on the contacts you've made. That extra day will come in *very* handy. If you're working a day job and the conference ends on Sunday, taking Monday off will also give you a shorter work week, allowing you a built-in break for breath-catching.

4.1.3 Travel

If you're considering a conference away from your hometown, you need to choose whether to drive or take a plane/train/bus. The positive factors involved in driving include convenience, relatively low cost, and having your car with you for errands, escapes, and editor tours. The negatives include parking (both as an inconvenience and an additional expense), time, and wear and tear on car and driver. The positive aspects of taking a plane, train, or bus include speed and low wear and tear on the writer. Negative factors include your costs and time for getting from whatever airport, train depot, or bus station to the conference. Another travel option you may want to consider is seeing if you could carpool with someone from your hometown to save money.

4.1.4 Lodging

After your registration fee (and, sometimes, before it), another of your biggest conference expenses will be lodging. If you choose a conference within commuting distance of your home (or if you happen to have friends or family with whom you could stay in the area of the conference), you can greatly reduce your out-of-pocket costs. If you have your heart set on attending a conference away from home and you have no available free housing, look into the accommodations offered by or on a university campus, either where the conference is being held or close by. On-campus dormitories or student housing are frequently available for a fraction of the price of a hotel room, especially if the conference is scheduled during summer break. Many conferences also offer double occupancy accommodations. If you aren't attending with someone you plan to stay with, talk to the conference staff about arranging a roommate for you.

If you're considering a large conference, you will want to reserve your lodging early so you won't have to spend half your conference day shuttling to and from an offsite hotel. Of course, if you *do* have to take a bus from the hotel to the conference and back, you'll naturally spend that time schmoozing with your fellow travelers, so it won't exactly be wasted. (More details in 11.12.)

4.1.5 Facilities

Is the conference taking place in a hotel or in a classroom setting? Why should you care? It all depends on what type of workshop/class sessions you're most interested in attending. If the sessions that interest you most are lectures or panels, so that your participation will primarily consist of taking notes and asking questions, either setting will probably work. On the other hand, if you are most anxious to take part in hands-on writing classes, where you'll be spending a large portion of your time with pen in hand, writing on the spot, you should make sure that some sort of desk or table surface is provided to help prevent terminal writer's cramp and wrist lock.

When you call or write for your conference information, be sure to ask these particularly important questions:

- *Is the conference taking place on a single floor/level? If not, how many floors are involved?*
- *Are there elevators available, or only stairs? How many stairs?*
- *How long is the interval between classes?*
- *Is the building fully accessible for those using wheelchairs or walkers?*

If you don't currently have any physical problems, you may be wondering why these points are important. Well, after two days or a week of running up and down stairs, even the most able-bodied writer can get tired.

Other, more general, questions you should ask include:

- *Does the conference site have designated smoking areas?* This is important to smokers and nonsmokers alike for obvious reasons.
- *How many people per classroom are they planning for?* You may not think the answer to this question will affect you. If you find yourself one of fifty people crammed into a classroom designed for thirty maximum, however, you'll really care—especially if you've been stuck standing through several other sessions. Depending on your

comfort level and the type of teaching you most need, a large conference with lecture-hall size classes may work just fine. If, however, you're as claustrophobic in crowds as we both are, you may prefer a conference that offers at least some smaller, more intimate classes.

- *Is there sufficient heating or air conditioning to deal with the number of attendees and the probable weather?* We were at a conference one very hot August on a college campus. There was no air conditioning, and the classrooms were so full of chalk dust that it was nearly impossible to breathe. Luckily, the campus design enabled most of the classes to simply move outside, under some shade trees. These conditions could have been disastrous for both the organizers and the attendees. Trying to take notes with frostbitten fingers isn't exactly fun, either. Ask the organizers if they've considered these comfort factors; if they haven't, they'll thank you for the reminder.

- *Are meals included in the registration fee? If not, what restaurants are available, how expensive are they, and what are their hours?* Meals can add a lot to your conference cost. Even if all meals are included in the registration fee, you should maintain some flexibility in order to be available for the contacts you will be making. It's also terribly important that some sort of coffee shop, cafeteria, or bar is available for those late night talk sessions. This is one of the most important places for you to haunt, even if you don't drink alcohol or coffee. You can always drink soda or juice while you're across the table from the editor you just bought a cup of tea or a glass of wine for. The editor will be grateful for the time and quiet—and the refreshment—and you'll both get off your feet for a while. (More about all this in chapter 11.)

- *If you're not staying in the same building in which the conference is being held, what is the parking situation at the site, and how far are you going to have to walk from your car? If you don't drive or prefer not to drive, is there a shuttle service, or reliable, affordable public transportation available? If not, what's the cab service like in the area?* Some conferences will offer shuttle service between primary hotels and the conference site, which can provide a great opportunity to meet other attendees and presenters. If you must resort to taxi service, figure this expense into your budget. Another alternative is to try to hook up with someone with whom you can split cab fare once you're at the conference. (More about this in chapter 11.)

4.1.6 Focus

Remember the questionnaire in chapter 3? This is where your answers start becoming useful. Read through the information available on the conferences you're considering. Then compare the curricula with the areas in which you need help or have the most interest. It won't hurt you if you attend a conference with some workshops that don't flip your personal switches, so long as there are enough classes that *do* interest you to make attending worth your while. At the same time, it's a good idea to attend a session or two on something you've never really considered before, since new perspectives and ideas may open your horizons and give you food for thought. And remember, all networking contacts have value, whether or not you can identify the value at the time the contacts are made.

4.1.7 Faculty

Look carefully at the listing of the faculty for each conference. Study the credits and experience listed for each instructor. Why was that person selected to teach? Go to your local library and do some preliminary research on the speakers, using reference books listed in the Bibliography. Figure out which combination of speakers and teachers can give you the most of what you need to learn. (This is actually a preliminary stage of the extensive research you'll be doing after you select your conference; more about this in chapter 6.)

4.1.8 Prerequisites

In reviewing the various conference listings, pay extra attention to any statements made about the expected attendees (or writers who've attended in past years). Are the conference organizers aiming for an experienced, professional audience, or are they focusing on beginners in the trade? Where do you fit in?

This is an important point to consider, since you don't want to waste your time and money on a conference that has nothing to teach you. But neither should you aim so high you end up too discouraged to continue. If the conference advertising or brochure doesn't offer you enough information, don't be afraid to call the organizers and ask questions. These people are offering a service to you for a fee. You have every right to verify that the service they're offering is the best choice for you. Questions to ask include the following:

- *Do they have résumés or demographics on former attendees? Would they send you copies, or at least provide you with a list or graph?*
- *Would they allow you to contact former attendees (with the attendees' permission, of course)?*
- *Do they have clippings from news coverage of the conference?*
- *What aspects of the upcoming conference have changed from previous years, and why?*
- *What level of writing ability and experience do they expect to reach in their classes?*
- *Where have they been advertising?* Professional or trade journals reach a different level of writer than newsletters distributed through amateur writing groups. A conference that advertises in a writing magazine you read regularly is a good choice for you to attend.

Once you have this information, gauge where you fit in terms of the criteria they've set.

4.2 Sift Your Information and Find a Match

Now that you've created a list of the conferences that interest you the most and which you think have the most to offer you, compare that list with your questionnaire results regarding your writing strengths, weaknesses, and interests. By weighing the offerings of your narrowed list against what you really need and want from a conference, you should be able to determine which conference is the right choice for you *this year* in terms of cost, location, and facilities, and offers the largest percentage of classes you need and people you should make contact with. (Keep in mind that by next year, you will have reached new heights and will need a different level of instruction.) Fill out your registration form, make your reservations, and mail your check. Then get ready for the *real* work!

5

Decide Your Agenda and Set Your Goals

NOW THAT YOU'VE REGISTERED for the conference (or conferences) you're going to attend this year, and you've received your agenda or registration packet, it's time to decide what *your own personal agenda* is going to be. While the conference organizers have worked hard to provide a wide selection of classes, lectures, workshops, or whatever form they're using, you're only one writer. You can't possibly attend everything any conference has to offer. In fact, you'd be crazy to try. Since you'll have only a limited amount of time and energy to invest in the conference, it's important that you choose carefully the pieces of the conference experience you want to participate in.

5.1 What Don't You Want to Attend?

The first thing we do when reviewing a conference packet (or a new market listing, for that matter) is to go through with a red pen (purple, in Lee's case) in hand and cross off the items we *know* aren't of interest to us. There's no point in spending your limited time on items that are far from your areas of current or projected interest. With us, this usually boils down to the writing areas of religion and poetry.

5.2 As Always, It Comes Down to People

Our next sweep through a conference listing usually involves circling the names of the speakers who interest us the most. Any conference is only as good as its people, and making "people contact" is always our primary goal in attending. So how do you go about deciding who can do you the most good? Ask these questions as you go through the conference catalog:

5.2.1 Who Can Teach You What You Need to Learn?

Pay particular attention to writers in your genre or area of interest, especially writers who are currently doing what you do or want to do, and are successful at it. They will teach you what you need to learn to climb the ladder they've already climbed, and they're great contacts for you to have.

In addition, if there's an area of writing or an aspect of the business side that you know you need to improve on, look for teachers who've published books or articles on that subject (ideally, books or articles you've already read and found helpful), or who have a reputation among other writers as being good speakers and teachers. How do you find out who has a good rep? *Ask other writers.* If there's a writer's organization in your area, whether or not you're a member (and if you're not, why not join?), call their office and ask what they know about the speakers you're considering. If they won't give you an opinion, ask for contact names and phone numbers of writers in your field so you can call and ask them. The writing grapevine is a strong communication link that you should be using. Start now.

5.2.2 Who Might Be a Contact You Could Use Now or in the Future?

Is there a magazine you've been dying to sell a story to? Look for that name among the credits of the conference speakers. If you find either an editor or a writer who lists that magazine in his or her background, circle that name. If you find a related or similar magazine listed in someone's credits, circle that person's name, too. Editors do talk to each other, and a contact with one magazine may well spawn a contract with another. If there is a book publisher you've longed to have look at your manuscript, see if any of the editors or writers mention a contact with that house. Making a strong connection with one editor (either in person or through a more established writer) can turn into a pipeline past the slush pile.

One of the wonderful things about the writing life is that writers, as a whole, are more supportive of others in their field than any other professionals we've dealt with. We sold our first two books as the direct result of personal contacts we'd made through conferences or writer's organizations.

A very good friend of ours, who has more than twenty science fiction novels to his credit, wrote a letter of recommendation to his editor on behalf of one of our writing students. Although our student's book didn't sell to that house, it pole vaulted over the slush pile and got as far as the marketing committee before finally being rejected. It gave that student a great boost of energy and hope for his future. And while it didn't cost our friend any more than some time to read the manuscript and write the note, he had to care enough about paying forward to do so.

In order to make things like this happen for your writing career, make all the contacts you can with writers who are publishing in your general field of interest. Impress them with your professionalism and your courtesy (and with your writing, too!). These contacts are quite likely to pay off in the future. If handled properly, this type of contact can provide introductions to editors or agents, either at the conference or later, possible introduction by letter at a later date, or tips on which markets might be open to your type of work at that time. The friendship possibilities just make the potential that much more interesting.

5.2.3   Whom Would You *Really* Like to Meet?

There's nothing wrong with being a fan of another writer's work. As a matter of fact, the first time we met that science fiction writer at a conference a number of years ago, Lee walked up to him after a panel and said, "Hi, there. I'm a *real* fan." We'd both read and loved his work, and were pleased to be able to tell him so in person. That "fannish" introduction has led to a very pleasant professional relationship and personal friendship. While most of our introductions to other writers have been considerably less gushing, every writer enjoys hearing that another writer is an admirer. There's also nothing wrong with walking up to another writer and admitting you haven't read any of his work, but would like to chat anyway.

The writer's grapevine is a valuable business tool, but it can't do you any good unless you're hooked up to it. Don't take everything you hear on the grapevine as gospel, but do listen and make all the contacts you can, particularly with writers in your field.

5.3 After People, Come Classes

After you've gone through the catalog and crossed out the areas you're not interested in and circled the people you're most interested in meeting, review the class and workshop listings one by one. Read each listing carefully, watching for areas of your particular interest. Once again, keep in mind that you can only attend one class per period. In fact, leaving yourself a planned rest period out of each day's work is also a good idea. Too many beginning writers (or experienced writers at one of their first conferences) set themselves up for failure by planning to duck into two or three workshops per period. *This just doesn't work:* It's exhausting for the participant, distracting to the other attendees in the class, and insulting to the instructors. It's also a waste of the participant's money, since he or she ends up attending everything and learning nothing.

Another important point is to be sure to allow yourself some flexibility. You'll need time to assimilate what you've heard, and time to catch your breath. It's also vital to allow yourself the option of flexing your agenda, since you may meet a writer or editor or agent that you *have* to spend some time with. Remember, you're at this conference to learn *and to make contacts.* If you lock yourself into attending workshops every moment of every day, you might just miss making the connection that could sell your next book.

5.4 Critiquing Services: Should You or Shouldn't You?

Conferences often provide critiquing services to their attendees, either included in the registration fee or for a small additional charge. Only you can tell whether this is something you need. If you wish to partake of this service, you'll need to include it in your timeline (and your budget, if there's a separate fee), since you'll probably need to meet with the writer/editor who performs the critique.

Once again, *who* is performing the critique will have a lot to do with whether it's of any value to you and your writing. If the critique service doesn't list who will be doing the critiques, talk to other writers who've attended the conference in the past and received critiques. Find out how they felt about the critique and the "critiquer." Some conferences make arrangements with experienced writers in their area to perform critiques for attendees; others use faculty writers and speakers.

Do you need to have your work critiqued at the conference? If you're writing in a vacuum (in other words, if you aren't a member of a critique group or writing class, and your circle of readers is most likely to say something like, "That's nice. I liked it"), this may give you some useful feedback.

On the negative side, whoever critiques your work at the conference will probably never see you or your work again (at least not until it's in print). This means you're getting one person's opinion with no follow-through. Whether or not this is a valuable way to spend part of your conference time and money is a decision you'll have to make. Take into account the time you have available, the money the service will cost, the stage your writing is at, and what (if any) feedback you're getting on your writing elsewhere.

A good friend of ours submitted a short story to the critiquing workshop at a conference several years ago. She was very excited about the idea, and pored over the writing samples she received from the other new writers who were to attend the workshop. She spent several hours writing very thoughtful critiques of the materials she'd received. When she arrived at the critiquing workshop, she discovered that the other writers had apparently seen fit to trash absolutely all the work they'd received, hers included. The professional writer who was supposedly running the workshop exercised no control whatsoever over the behavior of the others, who were allowed to rip to shreds both the writing and the writers.

Luckily, our friend had a sufficiently low center of gravity that she got out of the workshop, tracked us down for a cup of coffee with some sanity on the side, and didn't allow the bad experience to sidetrack her. Had she been less confident of her own work, or alone at a conference away from home and friends, that poorly run critique session could have ruined her entire conference experience.

The moral of the story: Ask questions before submitting yourself and your writing to strangers for critique. You have every right to know the backgrounds of the people who are going to critique your work, particularly if you have to pay for the privilege.

5.5 It's Party Time!

Most conferences include a variety of social functions, usually in the evenings after the workshops are over or around mealtimes. These can run the gamut from crackers and cheese in a hospitality suite to formal affairs hosted by international publishers. These functions provide wonderful networking opportunities—if you play your cards right. This is one time where the "drop in, check it out, move on" mode can actually work, with a few caveats.

If you drink, do so very sparingly. Alcohol is not inherently evil, but it will substantially reduce your ability to do business. A reputation as an irresponsible drinker won't do your career any good at all. If you don't drink, don't feel like you need to imbibe to fit in. Even if everyone around you has an alcoholic beverage in their hands, stick to your guns and drink water if you have to. Besides, empty hands are easier to shake with.

Frankly, these gatherings offer another feature that has served us (and many other first-time attendees or underbudgeted writers) well. Nearly every party will offer food. As long as you maintain some degree of subtlety, you should be able to at least hold off starvation by chatting your way around the buffet table at a few parties.

While you're dropping in on various social gatherings, keep a pocketful of business cards handy, and give them out freely. As you're giving yours out, be sure and get the other person's in return—every time, if possible. (See 8.2 and 9.7 for more details on business cards.)

5.6 Get Your Goals on Paper

Now that you've sorted through the classes, services, and activities offered by the conference and have a reasonable base of information, it's time to firm up your personal goals for the conference. Sit down with pen and paper and sketch them out.

5.6.1 What Do You Want to Walk Away With?

It may seem silly after all this preparation, but this is an important question. What end result do you want to achieve from this conference experience? If your main goal is to use the conference as a social function, fine. But don't be disappointed (and don't blame the conference) if you walk in expecting nothing more than socializing and walk out with no viable business contacts. If you want this conference to make you business contacts and eventual contracts, you must have that goal firmly in mind at the outset. Write your one-sentence goal at the top of your paper. Keep it in mind throughout your entire planning process.

5.6.2 Whom Do You Intend to Meet?

Since you've already gone through the conference literature in depth, you should have an idea of who is going to be there, at least as far as speakers and teachers are concerned. Which of those people do you want to meet, and on what level (professionally or socially, or both)? Do you plan to meet these people through workshops, or networking, or do you know another writer who can introduce you? List the people you'd most like to meet, with notes on how you hope to meet them. (We sometimes do an A and B list of people, so that when we have to make a choice between contact opportunities, we've already sorted out those people we most want to make contact with. Of course, being a two-headed writer comes in handy, since we *can* be two places at the same time!)

5.6.3 What Do You Want to Learn?

While you should definitely stay flexible so as not to miss out on unexpected opportunities, you need to have a reasonably firm idea of where your weaknesses lie and which weaknesses this conference can strengthen. Write down your primary learning goals, together with the classes and workshops you think will best educate you toward those goals. (It doesn't hurt to do an A and B list on these, too, since classes can fill up in a hurry.) If the conference allows preregistration, and there are courses that particularly interest you, get your name in early.

5.6.4 Which Services and Social Functions Should You Partake Of?

Last of all, jot down the services (critiquing, personal conferences, and so on) and social events (awards dinners, receptions, and so on) that you're interested in. Since services often include an extra charge, factor any cost into your decision. Keep in mind that the social functions are probably the most flexible aspect of your conference experience, since on-the-spot schmoozing and networking may well turn up greater opportunities than you can predict from a distance. And remember that cost does not necessarily equal value. At the American Booksellers Association convention in 1992, one of the most memorable events for us was the American Book Awards presentation ceremony. The ceremony was free, the refreshments were free, and it was a terrific dream-boosting session for both of us.

5.7 Ready, Set, Schedule!

With your notes in one hand and the conference schedule in the other, sketch out your personal agenda for the conference. Leave yourself room for an occasional cup of coffee and breath-catching stop. By doing so you should have a better chance of actually sticking to your plan, thereby achieving your goals and providing yourself with the best possible conference experience. At the same time, keep an open mind and a flexible clock, so that when that agent says, "You know, I've been looking everywhere for a murder mystery set on Mars," you can jump right in and buy her a cup of coffee while you pitch *your* Martian what-done-it.

6

Educate Yourself

YOU'VE REGISTERED for the conference, read through the literature, and sketched out your agenda and basic plan of attack. Ready to go, right? *Wrong!* All you've done so far is the most preliminary research. Now comes the *real* work.

6.1   Hit the Books

With your list of speakers, teachers, and advisers in hand, go to your local library and sit down with the current edition of the *Literary Market Place* (see the Bibliography for details). We don't suggest you buy your own copy for two simple reasons: it costs over $160 and is updated every year. (Thank heavens for libraries.) The *LMP* lists virtually every publisher in the country, including every editor, assistant editor, and so on down the line. Besides addresses and names, it also lists how many titles were published the previous year by a given publisher, how long the publisher has been in existence, which editors work for which imprints, and much more. Reading through the *LMP* is an education in itself, and one that we recommend to all writers. In fact, we still sit down with the new copy each year (borrowed from a publisher friend), and review the changes made over the past year that affect the publishers and editors we work with.

With the *LMP* in front of you, go through the publishers and editors in your list of names. Make notes of all the information available, including mailing addresses for postconference submissions.

While the *LMP* is the industry bible, of vital importance to every publisher, there are other books that are aimed more directly at the writer. Every writer should own current copies of at least *Writer's Market* or *Novel & Short Story Writer's Market*, depending on whether the writer is writing nonfiction or fiction (See the Bibliography for ordering information). (We actually own both and use them on a regular basis.)

These listings are important to marketing your work, although neither is infallible. (Writer's Digest Books also produces other, more specialized listings, including *Poet's Market, Songwriter's Market, Children's Writer's & Illustrator's Market, Mystery Writer's Market Place*, etc.; see the Bibliography for details.) Whatever your writing specialty, you really should own or have ready access to the current market listing for your field. These sources are a great place to start your submission process. They will also provide you with information on the market's needs, guidelines, length requirements, and tips. They will also help you gather information for your conference preparation.

6.2 Never Use Outdated Listings .

One important tip regarding market references: *Don't try to make do with an outdated listing.* People in publishing change jobs as the markets change and companies change hands. Someone who *was* an editor at Tor may now be at Walker & Company, editing an entirely different genre. Get the most up-to-date information, but recognize that it may be flawed, too. Even a hot-off-the-press market listing in book form contains information that's at least three (and more often six) months old. The listings are a great *starting point*, as well as a general information and education source.

You should also review any market listings for your specific genre or type of writing. While most of these listings are too limited to be your sole source, they may round out the information you glean from the other options.

There are also listings of literary agents beyond those mentioned in the *Literary Market Place*. Another option is the *Guide to Literary Agents and Art/Photo Reps* (see the Bibliography), which will provide you with submission information to add to your notes. While these sources won't list every agent in the business, they will offer you a starting place. However, unless you're going to have a scheduled personal consultation with an agent, and that agent specifically requests that you submit your work before the conference, *don't* submit! You may well find that you and the agent butt heads from your first meeting. Or, you may hit it off immediately with a *different* agent when you meet in person.

A side note on agents: We're firm believers in meeting or at least speaking by phone with an agent before we would consider being represented by that agent. The agent/author relationship is far too important to be left to a name on a page. We've been represented by three different agencies, all three of which became warm acquaintances *before* they represented us. While this is a luxury not always available to all writers, we recommend at least getting a feel for who the agent is, either in person or over the phone, before signing your career over to a stranger.

One other point: You are fully within your rights to request (*politely*) a list of the agent's clients and/or recent sales.

You do *not* have to approach an agent, hat in hand and begging. You have every right to ensure that the agent you're considering is truly qualified in your field and has actually made the sales he or she is claiming to have made. Ask around; check with other writers who may have more or different contacts and sources of information. Don't just blindly agree to sign with an agent you've never heard of before, just because the agent says okay. There are no licensing requirements for literary agents; somebody's brother-in-law can (and it's been known to happen) hang out a shingle listing himself as "Joe Blow, Literary Agent." Editors can spot these phonies from a mile off, but writers all too often fall for the ruse. Do your research. Ask *lots* of questions, and listen to your own instincts: Does this person sound like she knows the publishing business, or is she faking it? It pays to check out an agent before you invest your career.

6.3 *Update Your Information*

Another great section in your local library is the periodicals department. There, you can read back issues of *Publishers Weekly, Writer's*

Digest, Poets & Writers, WRITER'S Journal and *The Writer*. There are also genre-specific magazines, which can provide you with inside information on your particular field. These include *Science Fiction Chronicle* or *Locus* for science fiction or *Premiere* for the film industry. There are too many to list here for poetry. (See the Bibliography for ordering information on the magazines listed.)

Look through at least the last six issues of each of these publications that apply to your work. Note any changes in the information you obtained from the book-form listings you went through first. Since the magazines are published more frequently and have a shorter lead time, their information should be at least somewhat more up-to-date. Most industry magazines include some sort of "what's up" column about comings and goings of editors, recent sales of note (including which agent did the selling), and so forth. Pay close attention to these columns; take detailed notes of anything involving your genre, any of the editors or agents you're interested in, and any writers who will be speaking at the conference. It will make a great first impression if you can walk up to the current hotshot SF writer and say, "Gee, I read about your new five-book contract with Avon. Congratulations!" Writers like to have fans, too, and honest good wishes make a great introduction.

6.4   Sharpen Your Tools

If one (or more) of the people you intend to meet at the conference is a magazine editor, sit down at the library with at least the last six issues of that magazine. If the editor has only recently taken over control of the publication, reading the issues both before and after the change of editors can give you some insight into the editor and how she thinks. (You should keep in mind, however, that the prior editor probably purchased at least six months' worth of material that will appear after the changeover. Just because the name on the masthead changes, that doesn't guarantee the editorial slant has changed yet.)

If you can't find the magazine at the library, call university libraries in your area to see if they have copies of the magazine on hand. It's also a good idea to find out what magazines your friends and family subscribe to. Ask if you can borrow copies you're interested in.

We suggest you gain access to those last six issues of the magazine without buying them (unless you already subscribe). We're absolutely in favor of supporting the magazines you hope to write for. But if you're researching fifteen editors, purchasing eighty back issues can be a wee bit daunting, particularly when you're saving money for your conference trip. If another writer you know is doing preconference research at the same time, the two of you could join forces in gathering magazines, particularly where your lists overlap. Don't, however, try to use the other writer's research. You're different people and you'll notice different things. Just see if you can combine efforts in acquiring the magazines; then trade them back and forth as necessary.

If one of your A list people is an editor with a book publisher, go to your local bookstore and look at books published recently by that house (check copyright dates). Keep in mind that a book that just hit the shelves was probably purchased as a manuscript at least eighteen months before. Once you've identified books published by a particular imprint, look through the copyright pages and acknowledgments. A good editor's name will frequently turn up one of those places, although some houses don't list editors as a matter of course.

If you don't mind the long-distance charges, you might select the three books most closely related to your own work. Then, call the publishing house and ask who edited those books. A receptionist or assistant in the subsidiary rights department can usually provide this information, so you're not interrupting (and possibly annoying) an editor in the midst of a busy workday. You usually can ask for this information without giving your own name, so if they *are* annoyed, they won't have anyone to connect their annoyance to. If you can get this information, ask if the editor or editors are still with the company; if not, ask where they've moved to. Keep the call short. Then thank the person on the other end of the line and hang up. *Do not, under any circumstances, try to get the editor on the phone!* If you are unable to get the information, be sure to thank the person politely and hang up. All it's cost you is a bit on your phone bill and a few minutes, and it may be worth the effort!

6.5 *Ask Your Friends*

Now that you've gathered your list of names, start asking other people you know in the business for their opinions of the people on your list.

Your purpose in asking is *not* to try to get dirt on anyone, but to build a basic picture from the opinions and feedback you get. Other writers you know, as well as editors, agents, and writing teachers with whom you have a relationship, can (and usually will) tell you what they've heard about a particular person in the industry.

Take all such opinions with a grain of salt (and adjust the value of the information by *your* opinion of the person giving the opinion), but add the information to your notes.

6.6 Do Your Homework

Whenever possible, find and read at least some of the work of writers you plan to meet. We slipped up on this one a few years back, when a well-known Northwest mystery writer was speaking at a conference we were working on. We purchased one of her novels, but were too busy to read it until after the conference. As a result, we made no more than a nodding acquaintance with her in person, only to discover afterward that we *loved* her writing. We've since had the opportunity to meet her and make a slightly stronger contact, but we really blew it the first time.

Don't let this happen to you. Don't try to read a writer's entire body of work in two weeks, but do read at least one book by each of your major interesting parties before the conference. Every writer likes to know that someone out there reads his or her work. It's always nice to be able to tell people how much you liked a particular book, story, or article of theirs. And why.

One reminder, however: If you haven't read anything by a writer you meet, *don't fake it!* A writer can tell if someone has actually read a piece of work he or she is trying to discuss. Lying about it only makes you look like a fool. And since you're supposed to be trying to look *more* professional, not less, faking it just won't help. If you haven't read the writer's work, admit it. Then ask which piece the writer would recommend you start with. Writers have opinions on their own work. And telling them you want to read their work, but don't know where to start, is hardly likely to insult them.

6.7 Get Organized

Now that you've gathered all this information, get yourself organized so that you can use what you've learned. Carrying a notebook or pad with your notes categorized by person usually works pretty well, but assemble your materials in a form that's most comfortable for you. Don't try to carry so much with you that you can't balance it all. If need be, keep only a limited number of notes with you; stash the rest in your hotel room (or your car, if you're commuting from home), where you can refer to them between sessions. You should plan to keep your primary contact wish list with you at all times, with shorthand reminders of details to key off of.

By the time you've met fifty people in a day, you're going to have a problem remembering your own name and history, let alone a stranger's. Write it down, then use your notes. Refresh your memory *before* going into a class. This homework is going to make your conference pay, so you will need to organize it cleanly, legibly, and carefully. Be sure to leave room for updating your information with what you learn during the conference.

You should now be feeling quite a bit more prepared (and more professional), with your information organized and ready to use on the conference firing line. With just a few more pointers, you'll be ready to hit the ground running.

7

Questions You Should Never Ask and Why

MOST OF THE QUESTIONS in this chapter are intelligent ones, which ride heavy on the psyche of every new writer. They're questions whose answers could mean the difference between success and failure, if only they were asked in the proper circumstances.

Each and every question listed in this chapter, however, can be answered by simply reading this book and the others published for the express purpose of answering common writer's questions.

So, before you attend the conference, read this chapter so you can use the conference for the purpose it was intended: to fine-tune what you already know.

7.1 How to Avoid Asking Dumb Questions

If you don't want to appear as an amateur, think your question through before you raise your hand for recognition. If you answer "yes" to any of the following concerning a question you want to ask—don't.

- *Is this a general question that I could answer easily by doing my own research?*
- *Is this a question I would not want to have associated with my professional persona?*
- *Is this a question that will not enhance communication between me and the speaker?*

- *Is this speaker the inappropriate person to ask this particular question?*
- *Is this a question I've already heard asked (and answered satisfactorily)?*
- *Is this question one that might insult anyone?*
- *Is this question one that may adversely affect my career?*

7.2 Questions to Avoid and Why

7.2.1 How Do I Get an Agent?

It was the last session of a conference we attended several years ago, and everybody was tired. In a mixed panel of editors and agents, this question was asked (and, for the most part, gently ignored) five times in less than an hour, three of those times by the same unenlightened young writer. By the fifth asking, one editor apologized very graciously for how harsh he thought his answer was going to sound, then said, "Write your book. Make it the best book you can. Sell that book. Once you've sold it, you'll be able to get most any agent you want." This is great advice that will work in virtually any genre.

This doesn't mean you can't do the research and meet the agents and narrow down the field until you know whom you want to represent you and your work once the book is sold. It just means that you can and should do the baseline work yourself, *then* bring in an agent to handle the negotiations.

To take this process one step further, let's say you've written your book, submitted it to a likely publisher, and gotten a call from the editor saying she'd like to purchase the rights to the book. If you've done your homework, your response should be, "Great! If I can get your direct phone number, I'll get back to you in the next day or so." Write down the number, read it back to verify (since your hands are probably shaking pretty badly right about now), thank her for calling, and hang up the phone. You're now entitled to five minutes of screaming and jumping up and down. And please note that you did not commit yourself to any details of the sale over the phone.

Now, pick the phone back up and call either an established writer in your genre or field, with whom you've hopefully already made a networking contact, or the agent you've already picked out through your research. If you're calling a writer, tell the writer your tremendous news and ask him whom he would recommend as an agent. Count on it: Writers who've been in the business for a while know who is representing others in the genre. They are also likely to know who's making sales and who's not. And, lucky for you, virtually any established writer (at least all the ones we know) will be willing to offer suggestions on an agent.

In either case, once you reach an agent, tell her about your project and the offer you've just received. The odds are extremely good that either she will agree to represent you in the negotiations—and why wouldn't she? She'll be getting her commission without having to do the actual selling. Or else she'll recommend you to another agent who will agree to represent you. Voilà! You now have an agent.

7.2.2 I've Got Two Agents Interested in Me and My Work, and I Don't Know How to Choose Between Them. One of Them Has a Lot of Power and Prestige, but I Don't Think I'd Be a Real High Priority for Him. The Other Has Less Experience. I Think I'd Get More of Her Attention, but She Might Not Have the Contacts that the First Agent Has. Which One Should I Go With?

This question was asked publicly, with both agents present and on the panel, but not addressed to either. Not a smart question in this setting, because what this question said to this professional panel was that this writer didn't have the brains to figure out what he wanted. Sadly, it was a question very important to his career.

What he should have done was to ask several of the many professional writers and editors (but *not* other agents) attending the conference for their advice. In private. In general terms. With no names, not even the names of the agencies involved.

The writer would have maintained his favorable contact with the interested agents, established himself as a professional in the eyes of all involved, and, most likely, gotten himself an agent. He didn't. Both turned him down.

7.2.3 What Name Do You Write Under?

One friend of ours usually answers promptly with "Isaac Asimov" or some other great, but dead, science fiction writer. When the questioner looks perplexed, our friend explains that the reports of his demise are just part of his press packet, and are designed to boost sales of his books. (Our friend has over twenty novels to his credit, all under his own name.)

Our writing is published under either our two full names, like this book, or as "Lee Stevens," our usual genre pseudonym. What makes this question dumb is that, if you've done your homework, you already know what name a particular writer is published under. Not knowing, when you had plenty of time to do your research before the conference, is inexcusable and labels you as an amateur.

7.2.4 Where Do You Get Your Ideas From?

It always amazes us to hear a writer ask this question, since we won't live long enough to use even one percent of the ideas either of us has, let alone both. Working writers don't run out of ideas; they run out of time.

However, you *can* ask a writer where he got the idea for a specific story or character. One friend of ours who has written a number of highly weird novels and a few even weirder short stories, is often asked where some of his truly uncomfortable characters were born, particularly since, in person, our friend's a pleasant, intelligent individual with a wonderful, around-the-corner wit.

Depending on his mood, his digestion, and his audience, our friend's answers range from the straightforward to the offplanet, but the core of his response boils down to the same thing—from his imagination and from watching people. Any writer whose suspense derives from character spends most of his time watching and listening to *people*—the people around him, the people he sees during an average day on the streets of his hometown, the people from his past—just people. Whatever you write, if you aren't already learning from the people around you, start now.

7.2.5 How Can I Keep Someone Else from Using My Title (or Idea)?

You can't. Titles and ideas cannot be copyrighted. However, once you've put the execution of your idea on paper (or into your computer), under the most common interpretation of current copyright law, your finished execution of that idea (poem, story, novel, article, book) is copyrighted.

7.2.6 Did You Draw the Cover of Your Book?

The publisher, not the author, has the sole right to design the cover art that its marketing department thinks will best draw the customer's attention on a book rack. Often, the author doesn't have the slightest idea what the cover is going to look like until she has the advance copies, when it's too late to do anything anyway.

7.2.7 What's the "Secret Word"?

This question takes many forms, but what they all boil down to is something like this: "You're a successful author, and I know *you* don't get rejections anymore, so could you tell me what the secret is—the secret password that will get me through to the person who will buy my book?"

The fact of having sold a book, and having had that book perhaps make a profit, will earn you a slightly greater attention span when the editor sits down to read your next manuscript. *It will not sell your book.* Only good writing, professionally presented to an audience (editor) with a space on her list for a book like the one you're trying to sell, will sell your book.

There may be exceptions, but unless you're in Stephen King's league, you will continue to get rejections—no matter how many credits you have managed to amass over the course of your career.

7.2.8 Why Do Editors Hate New Writers?

They don't. But they do hate unprofessional behavior, bad manners, amateurish manuscripts, and other infuriating (and easily avoided) problems common to new writers. Do your homework and you won't be part of the problem.

7.2.9 What's Your Fax Number?

If an agent or editor offers you her fax number because she wants you to submit a proposal on a very time-sensitive project, great. If the agent or editor you're asking is someone with whom you already have a working relationship, this is probably a safe enough question. If, however, you are a new writer (or at least new to this relationship) and you ask this question, bells and whistles and warning signs go off in a big way in the agent or editor's head. *Under no circumstances should you ever submit anything to an agent or editor by fax unless you have that person's **express** permission to do so.* The industry is full of stories (like the one we heard once from a senior editor at a major paperback house) of writers submitting *entire novels* via facsimile. In the story we heard, the editor couldn't disconnect the transmission, and was stuck receiving a four hundred-page manuscript for something like eight hours. Needless to say, the novel was never even considered.

Also in the "never submit by this method" set: Federal Express, express mail, priority mail, UPS express services, and never, *ever,* **ever** by certified or registered mail. None of these will get you any quicker attention from the agent or editor; they all cost you extra money you don't need to spend; and in some cases (like most certified or registered mail), you'll be enormously inconveniencing the said agent or editor by forcing him to go to the post office to sign for your submission. This is a lousy way to start a business relationship, and a nearly certain way to guarantee that the relationship will never fly.

7.2.10 Why Can't I Sell My Writing?

This is an example of a question you should be asking yourself, not someone else. No one but you can change how you're polishing, proofreading, or preparing your work, or choosing the market that best suits your work, or selecting the editor to submit your work to, or reading the market listings and magazines to stay on top of the field, or finding the courage to remain persistent in the face of rejection. How can anyone else tell you what you've forgotten to do?

The next time you get a rejection in the mail, stop a moment and look at the piece of writing and the market to which you submitted it. Go back through the questionnaire in chapter 3. Then review this piece of writing against the questions there. Does your hook or lead (the first sentence or two) grab the reader and create the imperative that she keep on reading? Are your characters interesting and clearly drawn? Does your plotting make sense, within the parameters of the story? And so forth.

Look at your submissions list. Did you carefully select the publisher and editor that sent you the rejection? If you've done the homework we suggested in chapter 6, you should increase your chances of selling your work.

7.2.11 Don't You Have to Live in New York to Make It in Publishing?

Not anymore. Years ago, when cross-country communication was still slow, this may have been closer to the truth. But the world and publishing have changed. Today, where you live no longer matters.

8

The Right Tools for the Job

BY NOW, YOU'VE MANAGED to find all the information you'll need (at least all the information that's readily available to you), you've evaluated your status as a writer, you've chosen a conference to attend, you've picked out whom you most want to meet at the conference, you've selected the classes that are most important to you, you know what questions you shouldn't ask. But you're not ready to go—not yet.

All you've really done so far is lay out your groundwork. Now it's time for the real work to begin. It's time to gather the supplies, materials, and attitudes that you'll need to successfully work this conference.

And we do mean *work* this conference.

Every worker needs tools, no matter what the job. Fill your toolbox with the right stuff before you go to work.

8.1 *Professional Attitude*

The first thing you need to have is a strong, well-balanced, professional attitude. This is an invisible costume that we pull on over our egos—a writer's suit, if you will. When we wear our writer's suit, it covers our fears, our insecurities, and that unbidden feeling that someone at the conference is going to recognize that the emperor has no clothes—that we aren't really writers after all, but impostors trying to pass as writers.

We will each still stop in front of a mirror every once and a while, stare deeply into our own eyes, and say firmly, "I am a writer. A writer is someone who writes. I write, therefore I am a writer."

8.2 Business Cards

Business cards establish you as a professional. Business cards are a professional way for you to let someone know how to contact you. Unprofessionals scribble their names and addresses on bits of paper and cocktail napkins.

But, just like everything else in life, there's a right way and a wrong way to design business cards.

First, don't try to be cutesy. This is *business*. That means no titles like "world-famous author" or "writer extraordinaire." No logos like teddy bears, hearts and flowers, or quills. No colors except plain black, dark gray, or brown ink on a white, ivory, or light gray card.

Second, this is *your* business card, and the only thing *your* contact will have as a reminder of how to get in touch with you. Use a business name only if it is a bona fide business, you own the business, and its express purpose is the business of writing. If it does not meet all these criteria, *do not use a business name.* Your name belongs on the card (make sure it's spelled right; printers do make mistakes every now and then), your address (or post office box), and your telephone number. (See Figure A for a couple of straightforward business card designs that you're welcome to copy.)

Because you're keeping your card simple, there's no reason in the world that you should have to spend a fortune to get it made. While prices vary across the country, if there's an office supply store near you, you should be able to order business cards for under $15. The only catch is that you may have to wait a week to get your cards, so plan ahead. Worse comes to worst, you may have access to the little "instant business card" machines that have been popping up, where you can design and print forty-eight cards for around $4. They're not the greatest business cards in the world (and remember to resist the impulse to use one of their definitely cutesy logos), but they'll give you something with your name, address, and phone number on it.

Finally, do not, unless you absolutely can't help it, hand out a dog-eared business card. Carry a simple business card holder and keep it

Steven D. Spratt
1234 Main Street
Anytown, Oregon 97000
(503) 555-5555

Lee G. Spratt

1234 Main Street
Anytown, Oregon 97000   (503) 555-5555

Figure A.

stocked. Your card is your representative, and it has to look good. You never get a second chance at a first impression. (In 9.7, we'll discuss the etiquette of handing out your business cards.)

8.3   *Use the Right Submission for the Job*

As with any other job, different types of writing require different submission tools. Make sure that you're preparing the right type of submission packet for the writing you're doing (and be absolutely certain to enclose a SASE with any manuscript, submission, proposal, or query). All the pieces should comply with the details for manuscripts listed in 8.4.

8.3.1   Book-Length Nonfiction

Book-length nonfiction is nearly always sold on proposal; in other words, the book is sold before it's written. In the case of completed nonfiction books, you may wish to submit the entire text instead of a sample, but your submission packet should still include the rest of the materials listed below:

- *Chapter-by-chapter outline.* Approximately one hundred words about each chapter, explaining content and depth. (Even if you've already written the entire book, you should prepare a chapter-by-chapter outline or summary of the book.)
- *Sample text.* The introduction (if you plan to have one) and the first one or two chapters (roughly fifty pages). The sample should show the style and flavor of the rest of the book.
- *Author's bio.* A brief detailing of your education, background, professional experience (as it relates to the subject of your book), and any special qualifications you have for dealing with the subject. You should also mention any publicity experiences (appearances on TV or radio, lectures, and so on) you've had.
- *Publishing history.* Copies of published articles you've written and a list of publishing credits (including any financial and sales information on books you've written).
- *Market analysis.* Description of the market for your book, including general interest, trends, related clubs or organizations, similar (but not competing) books, and any review possibilities you foresee (related magazines, frequent media coverage, and so on).
- *Competition.* Any competing titles. Check in *Books in Print*, and talk to bookstore and library personnel. Tell how your book will differ from the competition (different angle, fresh outlook). If there aren't any books on this subject, explain why. Describe what will make this book more successful than the competition.

- *Extras.* Projected length of the book; number and type (color or black-and-white) of photographs, drawings, or other illustrations, and how you plan to obtain them; any supporting matter (appendixes, glossaries, and so on) your book will include.
- *Projected delivery date for completed project.*
- *Research and resources.* List any special groups or individuals whose help you have enlisted or plan to enlist.

8.3.2 Short Nonfiction (Articles)

Short nonfiction can be submitted either as a finished article or as a query letter. A finished article should be formatted much like the fiction manuscript described in 8.4. A query letter is essentially a miniproposal for an article. The query, which should ideally be no more than one or two pages long, should include the following points:

- *Description of article.* A catchy explanation of what you intend to say and how you plan to say it. Your passion for the subject matter, the particular focus you plan to use, and your targeting of the subject to the magazine's audience are the primary aspects you should cover.
- *Projected length of article, estimated time needed to complete the article, and any projected expenses.* Keep in mind the guidelines for the magazine you're querying. Don't project a length that doesn't fit or ask for reimbursement of expenses if the guidelines say they don't pay writer's expenses.
- *Clippings and/or list of publishing credits, if any.* Enclose copies ("clippings") of any articles you previously had published, or give a list of your publishing credits. If you don't have either of these, state why you are the best choice to write the article you've proposed— whether because of an avid hobby, or connection to your day job, or relevant college studies.

8.3.3 Book-Length Fiction (Novels)

In today's fiction market, it's virtually impossible to sell a first or even third novel on proposal; most publishers require a strong track record of novel sales before they will even consider a fiction proposal. Novels can, however, be submitted either as complete manuscripts or as a proposal packet whose components are listed below. If you're submitting a completed novel, your submission should include the full manuscript (instead of the sample) and the synopsis.

- *Synopsis.* A narrative summary of the novel, usually in present tense, either single- or double-spaced. Summarize either chapter by chapter, or do an overall narrative. The synopsis should include as much excitement as the project itself—and don't hide the ending. In order to do its job, the synopsis must include the high points of the plot, including how the book ends.
- *Outline.* A chapter-by-chapter sketch of the book, usually in far skimpier form than the synopsis and always single-spaced. How much detail you go into depends on you and your writing. Your outline, when combined with your synopsis, should give the editor a strong idea of what your finished book will be like.
- *Sample text.* The first fifty pages or so of your manuscript. These first few chapters must be the strongest you can possibly make them, even if you have to go back later and bring the rest of the manuscript up to this standard.

8.3.4   Short Fiction (Short Stories)

To submit short fiction, all you need is the completed manuscript (see 8.4 for formatting instructions) and a SASE. It's okay to include a cover letter if you have publishing credits to list, but don't try to summarize your story in the letter. Let your writing speak for itself.

8.4   *Your Manuscript*

If you're planning to bring manuscripts to the conference, please take those extra steps to ensure that you look good on paper. These steps are important because your manuscript represents you. It's your résumé and job interview all wrapped up together in one package, and it needs to look good.

Fortunately, it's not all that hard to rise head and shoulders above 90 percent of your competition. All you have to do is follow these few simple rules. Not following any of these rules can brand you an amateur, despite the professionalism of your writing itself.

8.4.1   Presentability

Your manuscript must always be typewritten with the pages numbered consecutively. One editor friend of ours tells a story about a manuscript she once received that was handwritten in purple ink on blue paper. This manuscript simply wasn't worth her while to struggle through. To top it off, the same day she received a note that read: "I have written a story that is perfect for you. Send me $50 and I will pay someone to type it." These are the writers who get automatic rejections because their manuscripts reflect the writer's unprofessional attitude.

8.4.2   Paper

Use white 8½ × 11-inch paper. **No other size or color is acceptable!** Use white computer or typewriter paper, preferably of at least twenty-pound weight. Never use erasable or thermal paper. If your pages tend to curl after printing (a common problem with laser printers), lay the stack out flat and set a large book on top of it for a while—a low-tech solution to a high-tech problem. And if you're using a dot matrix printer with continuous run paper, carefully burst (tear apart) the pages, making sure to remove all the tractor-feed edges. It's not the editor's or agent's job to tidy up your work.

8.4.3   Ink

Use a fresh ribbon or cartridge with black ink. Again, no other color is acceptable. You want to present clear, black type that's easy to read.

If you're using a computer and printer, be sure to go through the manuscript page by page to check the print quality. It's too easy with a computer printer to see that the first few pages look great, and miss the fact that your ink or toner cartridge ran out at page seven. The printer will keep on producing mostly blank pages, and you won't know unless you check.

Dot matrix printing is acceptable as long as the characters are black (not gray) and there are enough dots to make the letters clearly readable. A 9-pin dot printer may be cutting your margin for error a bit too closely, but a 24-pin printer with a fresh ribbon should be perfectly acceptable. Be sure to set your print quality to "high" and check your ribbon frequently to ensure legible type. Don't let your equipment cost you a sale.

8.4.4   Typeface (or Font)

Your manuscript should be printed in plain old 10-pitch Courier (or about 12-point type). Type, or fonts, is figured in either "pitch" (the old typewriter method, defined as number of characters per horizontal inch) or "points" (typesetting terminology, figured as 72 points to the inch). So long as you're using Courier, in either 10 pitch or 12 point, you should be fine.

Your printer can make fancy fonts and pretty effects, but don't use them. Editors want your manuscript to look like it was typed on a sturdy typewriter with a new ribbon. It's easier on their eyes and easier for them to read, and that's what they want.

8.4.5   Margins

All margins (top, bottom, left, and right) must be at least one inch. That means there must be at least one inch of white space between the type and the edge of the page on all sides. In the case of the top margin, that's one inch to the writer's name, address, and word count information.

8.4.6   Spacing

If fiction or nonfiction, your manuscript *must* be double-spaced—not one-and-a-half, not triple, but double. Double spacing makes your manuscript easier to read and edit.

If you're writing poetry, you have more leeway in spacing your work. However, be sure your manuscript is presented in the most professional format you can. If you're not sure about the proper submission format for your particular type of writing, check the books written specifically on manuscript formats. Also, the major market listings in the Bibliography usually include a brief description of proper formatting in their introductions.

8.4.7 Word Count

Here, too, you have some leeway. When we first started writing, our average page ran about 248 words. Several years later, as our writing began to run more heavily to dialogue, our word count dropped to an average of 218 words. Now most of our fiction runs closer to 235 words or so. The point is, depending on the dialogue-to-narrative proportion in your writing, anything from about 200 to 250 words per page works. If you find that you're running closer to 300 words per page, check your margins (which must be at least one inch on all sides), make sure your type is actually Courier (either 10 pitch or 12 point), and be sure you're in true double spacing. If your word count is running too low, your margins may be too big (although you're allowed some flexibility on the right, where you can go up to an inch and a quarter or so), your type may be too large, or you may be running triple space instead of double. Don't worry if your word-per-page counts vary in different stories, or even in the same story, so long as your overall average is about 200 to 250 words per page.

8.4.8 Proofreading

Check one more time for typos and misspellings. Get them all! Remember, you're hoping to give this manuscript to a person with the authority to buy. Don't blow it by getting sloppy in the home stretch. Don't make corrections on the paper, if you can possibly avoid it. Whether you've typed your manuscript on that old typewriter or printed it out with your new laser printer, it pays to retype or reprint any pages with corrections.

8.4.9 Format

We wouldn't ordinarily include this, assuming that any of you who are interested enough to get this far would already know how to format a manuscript, but we've seen too many "should-have-known-betters" foul up. This is a simple thing, but one you must know if you're going to get past first base with an agent or editor.

Figures B and C (reduced in size, of course) show how to prepare a fiction manuscript for submission. Here's how the details break down:

- *Name, address, phone number.* At the top left on the first page, print your mailing address, phone number, and (for short fiction or magazine articles) your social security number. Why is this latter information important? Look at it this way: You've so impressed a magazine editor with your writing that she's anxious to purchase the rights to the manuscript and write you a check. She can't write the check until she has your social security number for the magazine's tax records.

  For a book manuscript, whether fiction or nonfiction, the social security number is unimportant because a check can't be issued until a contract is signed, and the contract requires your social security number.

- *Estimated word count.* Most word processing programs can give you this number pretty easily. If you're not using a computer, or your WP program doesn't count words, here's what you do. For a short story, take three average-looking pages, and count every word on each page (excluding headers). Total the number of words on the three pages, and divide by three to get the average count. Multiply this average by the total number of pages in your manuscript, and round it up to the nearest one hundred words. Put this figure in the upper right-hand corner of your first page. For a novel, use the same process, but count five pages and average them.

- *Title (and name, if any).* The title is five inches down from the top of the page, followed by two line spaces (or one double-spaced return) below by the word "by," then two more line spaces and your full name. If you're using a pseudonym, print that name in place of your real name. If this were one of our genre manuscripts, the title would be followed by "by Lee Stevens." The story would then begin after four line spaces. If you're using your real name, you don't actually *need* to put anything below the title but the story. If you don't repeat your name, just print the title five inches down from the top of the page, followed by four line spaces, then begin the

Steven D. Spratt   About 1,300 words
Lee G. Spratt
1234 Main Street
Anytown, Oregon   97000
(503) 555-5555
555-55-5555/666-66-6666

JIMI

by

Steven D. Spratt
and
Lee G. Spratt

   He caught the phone on its first ring, irritably

snatching it from the cradle. "Doctor Hendrix," he

snapped into the receiver. He had cause to be

irritable. It was nearly midnight, and his

departmental budget report was due tomorrow.

Everybody likely to call knew this. He'd even sent

his family over to Eve's mother's for the evening so

he could get his work done.

   "Jimi?" The voice on the other end sounded

tentative, scared.

Figure B.

Spratt & Spratt/<u>Jimi</u>/2

It was the music in the background at the other
end that made the connection in his mind, Janis
Joplin poring her soul and about a triple shot of
Southern Comfort into "Cry Baby." Nobody like her,
before or since.

And nobody called him Jimi any more. Walter, if
they knew him well, or Doctor Hendrix, but never
Jimi. That was Scott's joke. He started it and the
others in the platoon just seemed to follow along,
calling their medic Jimi because of his last name.

"Jimi? That you, bro?"

"Scott?" Just uttering the name tore twenty years
of protective layers from his soul.

"Yeah, bro. One and the same."

"Where are you? You in town?"

"Yeah, bro, I'm in town."

Hendrix pushed the stack of papers away from him,
and swung his feet up onto the desk. "You are one
crazy mother, Scott. What the hell town are you in?"

"Detroit." Over a thousand miles from where
Hendrix sat in Atlanta.

"Well, you coming this way? It'd be great to see
you again."

Figure C.

story. In any case, the story begins four line spaces down from the title (and author or pseudonym, if any).

There are a couple of real-world reasons for this formatting style. In many magazine publishing houses, the white space on the first page of a manuscript is used for instructions to the typesetter. If you don't leave that room, you're inconveniencing your editor, which is a major mistake. In addition, as a writer and editor we know once pointed out, by having one or two paragraphs on the first page (in other words, the hook and maybe a little more), if you've done your job in setting your hook the editor will almost *have* to turn the page to see what comes next. And once you've gotten the editor to turn one page, persuading him or her to turn the next is substantially easier.

- *Follow page header.* The follow page header should have your real last name, the story's title, and the page number (see figure C). If figure C were taken from one of our genre manuscripts, the follow page header line would read: Spratt (Stevens)/Jimi/2. The continuation of the story then starts four line spaces down from the header.
- *And at the end of the story . . .* Type the word "END," centered, about four line spaces down from the last line of the story. *Don't* use "fini" or "30" or "-00-" or anything else, just "END" (or "THE END," if you prefer). While "30" is proper in journalism, it isn't proper for fiction or other nonfiction writing. "Fini" is proper *only* if you're writing in French. (See chapters 11 and 12 on how and when to give out your work.)

8.5   Other Supplies

So, you've got your business cards and you've got your manuscript all polished and ready to go. You're doing great. Now run over this checklist and make sure you have the other supplies you're likely to need.

8.5.1   Pens (Yes, More Than One)

Pens have a tendency to get lost. They're also programmed to run out of ink just when you need them most.

Be sure that the pens you're carrying aren't fountain pens or some other heavy ink writing implement. Fountain pens may be great for signing important documents or letters, but they're lousy for conference use. The ink is so thick that it bleeds through the average sheet of paper, and blotches when you least expect it. To prevent this, use medium or fine point felt tip or roller ball pens.

8.5.2 Paper

You'll need paper for note taking, and notes are essential—not just on the conference and its speakers, but for future story ideas as well. Buy good old reliable spiral bound steno pads or small legal pads. The paper is fairly sturdy (it's less likely that the ink will bleed through), the pages are easy to turn quickly, and the pads are small enough to be carried comfortably.

8.5.3 Proof of Registration

Mistakes can happen, particularly because volunteer organizations run most conferences, so be sure you're carrying whatever receipt or confirmation slip the organizers sent. Even a cancelled check for your registration fee can be sufficient proof that you really did preregister. Carrying this proof with you can also save you from any tantrums that you might be tempted to throw, thereby preserving your professional attitude and keeping your blood pressure in the safety zone. And remember to take that proof home with you, too, for your tax records.

8.5.4 Clipboard

This is certainly not a necessity, but trust the voice of experience: Trying to juggle a pad of paper that's down to its last two sheets while you're taking notes standing in the hallway is a great way to break your arm. A clipboard will give your tired arms and wrists the stability they need.

8.5.5 Laptop Computer

If you have a laptop, it doesn't hurt to take it along. Just remember, most laptop batteries are good for at most two hours, so turn off the laptop before it starts that annoying little "beep-beep-beep" that's trying to tell you you're running out of juice. We would also advise not using a laptop in a small, intimate workshop. You don't want to annoy the speaker by keeping your head down and never making eye contact because you're so determined to get down every word. Also, never take a laptop in place of paper and pens. There are simply too many situations in which either the group is too small for you to get away with the laptop, or the battery dies, or you're standing in a hallway trying to commit to screen a really important point the speaker made just before the end of the session.

We suggest you keep your laptop in your hotel room for writing opportunities, and stick to paper and pen for note taking. Besides, in the room, you can just plug the laptop into the wall and forget about battery problems.

8.5.6 Tape Recorder

Should you or shouldn't you bring a tape recorder to the conference? If you plan to use it to record notes to yourself, story ideas, impressions, and so on, then, by all means, take it along. But if you're thinking of recording the workshop sessions you attend, think again.

Many speakers at these conferences make a portion of their income from teaching and/or selling tapes (both video and audio) of their lessons. Taping these classes would be a violation of the speakers' right to earn income from the information they're sharing with you. *If you know the speaker fits into this category, under no circumstances should you even ask him if it is all right if you tape his lecture.*

There will be other speakers who choose not to be taped, because they're uncomfortable knowing that there's a tape recorder capturing their every stammer and hesitation. These people will not want to be taped.

Once in a very rare while, though, you may be granted permission to tape the class. Once you have this permission, then feel free to haul out your trusty little tape recorder and set it to spinning. We've found, over the course of the years, that it happens so seldom we no longer bother to bring along a tape recorder. Our advice: Leave the recorder home.

There's another reason for not tape recording class sessions at a conference. If you take notes on what a speaker is saying, you will be noting the points that are of interest to you. If, however, you tape record every word the speaker says, you will still need to go back through the tape at a later date. In other words, you're still going to end up taking notes, one way or another, if you're going to get any value out of the session. So why bother to go through the time, expense, and possible speaker annoyance of taping, when you can just take notes in the first place?

8.5.7 Briefcase or Book Bag

While a briefcase or book bag (preferably with a shoulder strap) isn't truly vital, it can sure make your life easier. Instead of having to juggle your pads, pens, notes, books, sunglasses, and tickets to meals or other events in your pockets and hands, having something to stash things in can simplify your conference day. Since Lee has arthritis in both hands, a bag with handles of some sort is absolutely essential; she can't carry much in her hands, but can carry a bag with a handle fairly easily. A briefcase or book bag can greatly improve your image, because it leaves you free to shake hands with people. If you do use a briefcase or book bag, *don't* carry your business cards in the bag. Carry your cards in either a shirt or jacket pocket, and save yourself the embarrassment of shuffling through the bag's contents when asked for a card.

There, you've done it! You've completed all the major steps necessary to prepare for a conference.

Now, it's time to take care of *you*. Before leaving for the conference, get a good night's sleep. Eat. Take your vitamins. Rest. You're going to need your strength.

Part Two

During the Conference

9

Present Yourself Professionally

You've got your homework done. You've made sure to get a good night's sleep. It's time to put this show on the road.

9.1 Cleanliness

You're going to be in close quarters with lots of other people for up to fifteen hours per day at the conference (and likely for several more hours in the evening), so even the most fastidious among us has to be extra careful. Always try to look and smell like you're just out of the shower, hair and nails clean and neatly groomed, the works.

9.2 Clothes Make the Writer Comfortable

Clean, casual, comfortable clothes and shoes are in order. Your clothes should represent your own sense of style and personality, but remember that you may have to sit on the floor during some more popular sessions. Something that makes you stand out from the crowd a little can work to your advantage. You'll also spend a lot of time on your feet, so pass on those spike heels or tight dress shoes.

Find your *own* sense of style and use it to your best advantage. What that sense of style consists of is entirely up to you. Choose something that helps you express not only your personality, but your sense of your business self—something that is uniquely yours and communicates your own individuality. For example, we both wear hats. Of course, it helps that we both like hats, we look good in them, and in Portland, it's a good idea to keep your head covered, because the chances are, it's going to rain sometime during the day. One of our publishers even insisted we wear our hats for the back cover photo on our short story collection, *Scars*, because they've become our trademark.

9.3 For Women Only

Think *very* carefully about what you wear to a conference, on both your body and your face. Heavy makeup may look great by candlelight, but you're probably going to be seen primarily in daylight and under fluorescents. That's not to say you can't or shouldn't wear makeup; wear whatever is going to make you most comfortable. But keep in mind those dreaded fifteen-hour days. Sweat is tough on makeup, and unless the conference you're attending is one of the few with really great air conditioning, you're going to sweat.

The same consideration should go into what you do with your hair. Wear your hair in the most comfortable and most professional style you can, and then leave it be. Fussing with your hair in public is unprofessional. Tweak your look in the rest room, but aim for the least conference time wasted in your overall appearance.

9.4 Get Your Mind Set on the Way

On your way to the conference, prepare yourself mentally for what is to come. As we said earlier, *luck is where preparation meets opportunity.*

Think about that for a moment. If you've followed our suggestions, you've accomplished the greatest part of your preparation, and you're on the way to grab opportunity by the horns at the writer's conference.

Now you can use your travel time to prepare yourself for what you're going to do with all the work you have done up to this point. This is your time to calm yourself, so that when you arrive at the conference, you're ready to hit the ground running.

9.5 Manuscript Dos and Don'ts

First, if you take one or more pieces of your work with you, leave it in the car or in your room. In all probability, *you will not have the opportunity to hand this work to an editor or an agent.* And you shouldn't even try.

The reason for this is very simple. Most editors and agents fly in for conferences, and taking an envelope from you would mean that they would have to pack it up and take it back with them on the airplane. One piece of work wouldn't necessarily be a problem, but multiply that by the number of people at a conference, and it could become a major problem of logistics.

Also, these people are at the conference to work. They put in at least as many hours as the attendees. Over the course of a conference, they will speak with at least a hundred people a day, most of whom have the idea of placing their work with an agent or an editor. Every single one of these people is likely to have at least one project they think is right for this agent or this editor. Think about it. Over a three-day conference, that could mean these agents and editors are offered three hundred pieces (assuming only one per person). Give 'em a break. But be alert. Sometimes opportunity does meet preparation and breed luck, and an editor or agent asks to see your work on the spot. Be ready to run to your car or your hotel room to get it for her— but *only if she asks.* Deliver it to her, whether at her room or in person (whichever location she specified) and *do not overstay your welcome!*

If an editor or agent is interested, he will ask you to mail your work to him. When this happens, make sure you have the accurate mailing address, and find out if you should address the submission to him or an assistant (verifying the spelling of the assistant's name, of course). If he doesn't ask you to send it, that does not necessarily cast an unfavorable light on you or your writing. It could mean he isn't interested in your project at this time, he doesn't handle your type of project, or he's so inundated that he can't consider any more new writers right now. Remember, *send your work only if you are asked.*

One agent we know attended a conference in the Northwest a few years back. During the course of the four-day conference, he asked three writers to send him manuscripts. In the month following the conference, he received *over four hundred manuscripts.*

In the case of the three manuscripts he'd asked for, he believed that there was a possible combination of writing skill and personality he could work with. Now he was left with the awesome task of rejecting eight hundred pounds of unwanted paper. And he refused to ever again attend that conference as a speaker. Who could blame him?

So, realize that you will almost certainly not be asked for your manuscript on the spot at the conference. Realize that when an agent or an editor asks for your manuscript, she is showing a definite interest in you and your work. And also realize that when an agent or editor does not ask you to send your work, or even specifically tells you not to send your work, he has a reason that quite often has more to do with his angle on the business than on your personality or writing.

9.6   The Great Business Card Exchange

Check your pocket or purse. Make sure your business cards are where you can get to them easily, so you seem as much of a professional as possible. Store them so that they will come out of your pocket face up, to save even more time and fumbling.

When you meet someone new at the conference, whether an agent, editor, another writer, or another attendee, do your best to exchange business cards at some point during the conversation.

Now, if this is an *important* conversation (read that as a conversation that may directly affect your career) and you want this person to remember what it was that you talked about, stop and make a quick note on the back of your card. Write down the gist of your conversation, perhaps the title of the project you discussed or a one-sentence description of the plot as a brief reminder of your conversation, before handing over your card.

Here's your chance to stand out from the crowd once again. A few words to jog the memory may be all that it takes for them to call you back.

Ask for their card, too. Most people will be quite happy to give you their card, because they, like you, are at the conference to do business. Just as they represent an opportunity for you, you represent an opportunity for them. However, if for some reason they don't want to give you a card, or have run out, don't panic and *don't* be rude. If they choose not to give you a card, thank them politely for their time and move on. If they've simply run out, smile in sympathy and either offer them a piece of paper on which to write their address information or ask for the information and write it down yourself. This is a great time to show off your professionalism and make a good impression.

Pay attention to the conversation. Listen for the details and the nuances. After the conversation is over (and we do mean *after*) and you are out of sight, take a moment to jot down a few reminder notes for your own use on the back of *their* card. Once again, it's a tool to provide you with accurate information—so use it.

There are a couple of exceptions to our "wait 'til after" idea about taking notes during a face-to-face conversation:

1. If the person you're speaking with is giving you *specific information* (names, addresses, markets, and so on), write the information down immediately and read it back to verify its accuracy. There's no reason to take a chance on a "write-o" that could blow a personal contact for you.

2. If you don't trust your memory, or you're feeling too scrambled to remember reliably, make discrete notes during the conversation, but be sure to maintain eye contact with the speaker as much as possible. If you keep your head down while you're scribbling, it's difficult for you to continue the flow of the conversation and it can be annoying to the person you're speaking with. Look up frequently, ask questions, but don't interrupt.

9.7 Speak Up

Speak clearly and concisely. To the listener, your speech patterns reflect your thought patterns. Your thought patterns reflect your writing style. You may not blather on the page, but if you blather in person to agents or editors, you will likely never have the opportunity to show them the difference.

Another point that we shouldn't have to bring up, but do, is this: *Speak up.* Lee has worn a hearing aid since her late twenties, so we're both aware of the speaking volume of other people's voices. It will do no good for the impression you're trying to make if the editor, agent, or writer you're chatting with has to continually ask, "What did you say?" It's frustrating and a bit insulting to the listener, and it's damaging to you. And if you chew gum, get rid of it before you corner a speaker for private conversation. Gum chewing makes your speech nearly unintelligible, and if your listener, like Lee, reads lips to supplement her hearing, gum chewing can really scramble the circuits.

9.8   What Is Your Book About?

At some point during the conference, you are likely to be asked, "What's your book about?"

If you're about to say, "Well, gee, it's about this guy, you see, and he robs a bank, and then he has a lot of adventures, you know, and there's this other guy, and he's a cop, see, and he's chasing the guy who robbed the bank, and then there's the bank robber's girlfriend, and they do some really interesting stuff before the cop catches up with them, and then the cop shoots him and he dies, the end," *don't*. This is a very important question, with a very specific type of answer required, and if you blow your answer, you may well blow your contact.

The first time an agent asked us this question, we were caught absolutely flat-footed. Luckily, we knew our story, even though we were still in the early stages of writing the book, and we managed to bumble our way through.

Later, after we had already bumbled our foot into our mouth, we found out that this was a standard (albeit fairly new at that time) way of screening writers. Up until then, nobody had ever warned us.

This may be the most important question you will be asked during the conference. It shows that the agent or editor is interested enough to ask the question, and gives you the opportunity to present your project in very short, very concise terms.

We used nearly three minutes to describe a book that finished out at about 75,000 words.

We found out later that day that what the agent was looking for was *one sentence*—one clearly stated, highly intriguing, easily understood sentence. When we went home that night, we spent over an hour trimming our description down to one sentence, and when we saw the agent again the following day, we presented him with our one sentence. He was pleased, and the repairs to the budding relationship were made.

We also learned *why* he wanted a one-sentence answer. Simply put, if he decided he wanted to take on the project, he needed to be able to describe the project to an editor, who would then (if she was sufficiently intrigued) eventually need to describe the project to the editorial board. The more concisely we could do this, the better the agent's chances of selling the project to editor, and the better the editor's chances of selling the project to the board.

In Hollywood, this is known as the "high concept"—a one-sentence encapsulation of the plot line of a book, movie, play, and the like. (If you've seen Robert Altman's enormously entertaining movie, *The Player*, you've seen high concept taken to its hilarious extremes. Remember Buck Henry discussing various movie combinations?)

Over the past five years or so, the idea of high concept has bled over into the publishing world, primarily because of the steadily increasing time pressures on the editorial side of publishing. If an agent is speaking by phone or over lunch with an editor, the agent needs to be able to pitch several projects at once. If she has to spend three or four minutes on each project, the editor's going to run out of time and hang up before she's gotten to the third project. If, however, the agent has a one-sentence high concept description for each project, she can hit the editor with a whole handful in a short span of time. This saves the agent time and the editor time, and can eventually make you sales and money.

So speak concisely. Speak clearly. Often, this is the only method an agent or editor has to judge the potential of you and your work.

9.9 Honesty Is the Only Policy

In the process of speaking, be honest. *Do not overinflate your credits or your knowledge.* If you do, the lie will come back to haunt you. Credits are checkable. Knowledge (or its lack) will show up on the pages of your work. You can't lie, even a little bit, and get away with it. Whatever you're tempted to lie about, it just isn't worth it. Guaranteed.

The other side of the coin is just as important. *Don't be overly modest.* That's just another form of dishonesty. This may be your only chance to sell yourself (to this person) as a writer. It's okay to blow your own horn; just make sure the music is true. If you already have credits, mention them—accurately. Publishing is a very small universe, and most of the players know one another. It's not all that hard to make a phone call to check out someone's credits.

If you don't have any credits, that's okay. Don't be embarrassed by your (temporary) lack of publishing credits. Everybody who has ever made the best-seller's list started out with no credits, and every agent or editor in the world goes to sleep at night dreaming about finding the next great writer, the next best-seller. It's words on the page that will gain their attention, and it's words on the page that will eventually gain you the credits.

So tell the truth, but tell it in such a way that you sound as good as you really are. Sell yourself as a writer. Sell your writing.

10

You've Arrived; Now What?

YOUR MOMENT has arrived—and so have you.

You walk into the registration area at the conference site, and into the middle of a mass confusion that reminds you of old movies about the preparation for D-Day. It seems like nobody in the room either sees you or knows what on earth is going on.

You're not all that far from the truth. Conferences are often staffed by volunteers who have had little or no training. They are frequently run by other volunteers who actually do know what they want to see happen, but are so busy coping with all the myriad little problems that always crop up at the worst possible moment that they have no time to give attention to making things happen.

You basically have two options: Either join in the confusion and have fun with it, or flee the room. We'd recommend that you join in the fun of it—even lend a hand if you see the opportunity. Helping out is a great way to meet people and create a good impression—as long as you don't lose track of what you came here to do.

10.1   The Art of Careful Volunteering

Be careful about offering to help. Listen to the things going on around you. When you hear something like, "Can somebody give a ride to (insert the name of an agent, writer, or editor from your list of people you want to meet)? He's stuck at the hotel."

If you have your car with you (or if there's a car you know you can borrow), jump on it! Get your hand up in the air, and make some noise. Get some attention. Jump up and down if you have to, but volunteer! (We have seen a few writers get carried away on this one, forgetting that they had no car with them, but volunteering anyway.)

You won't find a better opportunity to meet this person, and create a (however minor) debt of gratitude. And it works. *Really* well. By using this tactic, we have both sold an agent on representing us and sold a book (two separate incidents, two different conferences, same basic maneuver).

Give the agent a ride, and you have him as a captive audience for the duration of that ride.

Give the editor a ride, and you have her attention on you, as an individual, for the duration of that ride.

Here is your chance to both create a friendship and present yourself and your work, in an atmosphere that is relatively relaxed for both of you. However, you needn't feel the urge to play tour guide, unless your passenger seems interested in hearing about the local sights. Also, don't feel you have to fill every moment of silence with words; allowing a speaker some quiet travel time to gather his thoughts for the day ahead, or recognizing that he may be too tired for chitchat by the end of a long conference day, will impress him more than any prepared speech you could possibly give. Be sensitive to the needs of your passenger, and keep your best professional foot forward.

Sure, editors and agents are perfectly capable of taking a cab and adding the fare to their expense account, but since they are here for business, they'd much rather get a ride from somebody who might just prove to be the next great writer for their list. The favor works both ways. You each get an opportunity you might not have had without your volunteering the effort.

If you hit it off—and the chances of that happening are greatly improved by the homework you've done—tell them that you'd be happy to give them a ride back to the hotel later if they need one (or to take in the sights, or to dinner, or to . . .).

No need to push it. If the click is there for both of you, your passenger will be most happy to take you up on your offer, since it will guarantee her a ride between the hotel and the conference, and give her one less thing to worry about. Stay attuned to her whereabouts during the conference if she has agreed to let you chauffeur her around, since she may need an escape route during the day. And if her answer was "no," thank her anyway, go back to square one, and keep your ears open.

10.2 Back at the Registration Desk . . .

As soon as it is practical, get back to the registration desk and get checked in. Make sure the conference organizers have your name spelled right and your address and telephone number are correct, in case somebody (like an agent or editor) wants to track you down through the conference attendance roster.

While you're at the desk, inquire about any last-minute changes in the schedule or the speaker list, and update your itinerary as necessary. Ask how often they intend to update the changes to the speaker roster and where those changes will be posted; make it a point to check back as the conference gets under way.

This is important! Not only will it keep you from showing up at a class or lecture that isn't going to happen (thus saving you from wasting your time); it will make you available to volunteer to transport late arrivals.

If there are any problems with your registration, stay cool. Any problem in your registration is just as much a problem for the conference volunteers as it is for you. Moreover, it's just one problem for you, but may be one of several dozen for them. Work with them to get the problem straightened out. Show them your documentation. Help them get it right. They'll thank you for it, and they'll remember it later if you need some extra help on another problem. (See also 8.5.3.)

10.3 Where Am I?

After you've registered, take the map of the facility in hand and do a little exploring. This is your time to relax and acquaint yourself with your surroundings.

Find out where the classrooms are and the fastest route between them. You'll likely need this information once the conference is in full operation. The time between classes is usually just barely long enough to make it from one to another—if they aren't too far away.

A WesterCon we attended one year was marked by the appearance
of t-shirts that read, "It's in the other hotel." It seemed that no matter
what configuration of classes we chose (or anybody else chose, for that
matter), our next scheduled class was always in the other of the two
hotels hosting the conference. Everybody got tired, most everybody
was late at least part of the time (speakers included), but everyone
managed to keep a sense of humor about it. Good advice for you to
remember.

If you have any problem dealing with crowds or claustrophobia, like
us, you'll also want to know where you can easily get outside or at least
away from the crush of people. It sometimes helps to be able to step
away and catch your breath for a moment. You can then step back into
the fray, refreshed and ready to roll.

There's another reason for knowing the layout of the site inti-
mately, and this one directly affects your business, the business of
writing. Watch for those people wearing instructor name tags. It's
probably their first time in this building, too. And they can get just as
lost as anyone else. (Did we see a light bulb go on over your head?)

Lend a hand if they look lost or like they're carrying more than they
can handle. They'll be grateful for the help—and maybe grateful
enough to lend a hand in return. Once again, this is just good manners
in practice, but being polite and helpful can really pay off in dollars
and cents.

Aside from the classrooms, and quite likely more important in the
grand scheme of things, learn the location of the common areas such
as the restaurants, bars, and rest rooms.

The restaurants and bars are the most important. While knowledge
is gained in the classrooms, business is almost always conducted in the
restaurants and/or in the bars. You need to know where they are, what
they're called, and how late they're open, because you may need to set
up business meetings with agents and editors, where you will be able to
talk with them, one on one, about your work.

10.4 Back Patting Break

You are now more prepared for this conference than 90 percent of the
attendees, and probably at least half of the speakers and over half of

the volunteers. Take time to pat yourself on the back for a job well begun.

10.5 It's Showtime, Folks

Now it's time to put all your concentrated effort to work for you. Make it to your first class at least five minutes early if you can, so you can get a seat front and center.

Front and center is the best place to draw that attention. You're in the speaker's face—right where you want to be. (It will also help you see and hear what the speaker's doing more easily.)

Take out your note pad and a couple of pens. Check to make sure that both pens work. Take a few seconds to reread your notes on the speaker, as well as the information on the class and the biographical notes contained in the conference booklet, to make sure that all this information is fresh in your mind. If you have a list of specific information you want to obtain from this speaker, take that out and go over it quickly, too.

When the speaker comes into the room, if she's not already there, *make eye contact and say "hello."* Use her name. If it seems appropriate to welcome her to the conference, do so. Let her know that you appreciate the fact that she took time out of her busy schedule to come to the conference.

Is this kissing up?

To a certain degree, yes, but not radically so. It is much more the establishment of a working relationship—and perhaps a friendship. It's opening yourself up to a business contact that might make a huge difference to your career.

10.6 A Note on Notes

Are you a note taker by nature?

If you aren't, the time has come to change your nature. We guarantee that every speaker will have at least one item of information that will be of vast importance to you, even if it's only an attitude you know you don't want to foster in yourself.

On the other hand, some speakers will seem as if they are speaking directly to you and addressing your concerns as if you had given them a list to prepare their class from. They'll seem to pick your questions from your mind and deal with them directly. For these gems, you'll want to take fairly detailed notes. But as you're doing so, remember to keep looking up and making eye contact. Nodding and smiling to show you're paying attention wouldn't hurt, either.

The vast majority of the information you'll hear will be of basically three types:

- Information you need right now
- Information you may need at a later date
- Information you will (probably) never need

For years, we wrote only fiction, so we listened particularly for information we could use to further our career in writing fiction. But we knew that it is very difficult to make a living as a fiction writer, so we also listened to the information on writing and selling nonfiction— both for the places where the information crossed over, and for what we knew would be an eventual need as we progressed to writing non-fiction.

The information we used to compile and write this book, to sell this book, and to promote this book was all gleaned out of classes we attended that were outside the normal flow of what we were interested in at that time. We wouldn't have made the sale or gotten this book published if we hadn't taken in this information and stored it for later use.

So take notes on both the applicable and the inapplicable (as you see it at this time). And take notes on anything you think you *may* need later in your career.

As we mentioned in 8.5.6, note taking is a precise way for you to keep only the information relevant to your situation. Taking notes on paper also eliminates the potential for alienating speakers.

10.7   Ask Questions

We've all heard it said that there is no such thing as a stupid question, and to a great extent, that's true. The exception to the rule is this:

Don't take up class time for a question you could have (and should have) looked up in a book during the course of your research. (See chapter 7 for our sampler of questions that are sure-fire ways to annoy a speaker.)

Why? Conferences are tightly scheduled. The speaker is encouraged to impart as much information as possible in as small a time block as practical. You, and nearly everybody else, are there to pick the speaker's brain, to gather as much of the speaker's own particular expertise and knowledge to yourself as you can.

One of the major differences between a professional and an amateur is that a pro asks questions that pertain to the speaker's subject matter, questions that can't be answered anywhere else, while an amateur asks lazy questions.

You've just spent the past several weeks gathering information and preparing yourself to act professionally in a professional setting. Why on earth would you open your mouth and declare to the world that you are just another lazy amateur?

So do yourself a favor. Check the list of questions in chapter 7 that are a no-no, and ingrain it into your very being that you *will not* be the one (often more than one during the course of a single class) to open your mouth and declare to the world that you don't know what on earth you're doing.

Take the time, your own time, to do your own research. Check the Bibliography to get started on what you need to know. *Read the books!* Learn from them.

Should you ask questions? Yes. Definitely. Ask questions when you don't understand what the instructor is saying. Ask questions when you don't feel the speaker has provided you with the information you want and need. And ask questions when you think the instructor is trying to get to something, but is struggling with it.

Every good instructor welcomes questions from the class. It makes her job easier, and it shows her that the students are paying attention. But don't waste her time—or yours for that matter—with questions that you could have (and should have) looked up in a book.

10.8 Watch for Chances to Visit with Speakers

We know that we stressed the necessity for you to set your own agenda as the blueprint for achieving your goals at this conference.

It is not, however, to be carved in stone.

It can and should be changed at a moment's notice to accommodate opportunity. If a speaker, especially an agent or editor, looks tired at the end of a session, or even while in the common areas between sessions, this is opportunity knocking. Often, he's tired enough from being on his feet so long, from being *on stage* for so long, that he would welcome the chance to just sit down, put his feet up, and indulge himself with a cup of coffee or a cold drink.

This is opportunity. Strike up a conversation with him. Tell him that he looks like he could use a break from the pace of the conference, a chance to just relax for a few minutes. Offer to buy him a cup of coffee or a cold drink.

Once you get to the bar, or the coffee shop, or the restaurant, or another common area, suggest that he sit down and hold a table while you fetch the refreshments.

What do you talk about?

Use some of your homework to compliment the person on a book he has edited or agented. Or an imprint he handles. Or the first book he was involved in. Or, best of all, a book he wrote or worked on that had a positive effect on your writing. You've done your homework on this person for a reason, and now's the time to let him know that you put out the effort to find out about him.

He'll be flattered. You will have shown him an all-too-rare professionalism that will lift his spirits like a spring breeze.

One other important point to remember is that nature abhors a vacuum, and human nature is to fill the vacuum of silence with words. This is a trap, so don't fall into it. Learn to use silence to your advantage. *You will learn far more with your ears open than with your mouth open.* Drill this into your head. Practice it until it is your nature to speak only when you have something to say and keep quiet when you have something to learn.

11

Making Contacts

THE MOST IMPORTANT ASPECT of any writing conference is people. And, the best thing you can do for yourself, your writing, and your writing career is to meet the people best situated to help you improve your art, your craft, and your bank balance. If some of these acquaintances eventually turn into friends, you've truly accomplished something.

11.1 Schmoozing, a.k.a. Networking

Quite a while before the current term "networking," we were using our own variation for what we do at a writer's conference, meeting, gathering, reading, or any similar function, including running into a fellow writer on a street corner. We called it "schmoozing," and defined it as the "fine art of creating friendly business opportunities."

Although we are both fairly shy, we still managed to walk up to people important to our career and talk to them as equal human beings. Part of how we did this was by "pushing the writing button." We learned to behave professionally in a schmoozing or networking situation, no matter how terrified we might have been on the inside, and regardless of whether we were alone or working together. We learned the lessons of our trade well enough that no matter who the person was, no matter how well known or famous they were, we could walk up and talk intelligently with them. We made plenty of mistakes (doesn't everyone?), but we tried to recognize that we were human and mistakes were part of the learning process. We learned from our mistakes and moved on.

How did we do it? In part, by recognizing that all the writers, agents, editors, publishers, and other experts with whom we wanted to make contact were human, too. They got tired after standing too long; they got thirsty; they got irritable and cranky on bad days; they usually had sunny dispositions on good days. Nobody told us any of this; nobody taught us how to do it. So we had to figure it out over far too long a period of trial and error. Good instincts saved us some time, and business backgrounds saved us some more, but mostly it was hard work.

In a conference setting, you can't depend on the right editors, agents, and other contacts finding you; you need to find them. But how do you make a personal impression when you're just one out of the hundreds of writers at the conference?

11.2 *Great Business Opportunities Are Made, Not Born*

Don't wait for opportunities. How and where you spend your free time at the conference can make all the difference in the world. If you have just a few minutes between sessions, instead of sitting in the classroom waiting for the session to start, stand out in the hall. If someone walks by whom you've been dying to meet (and that someone doesn't look like he's running desperately for the rest room), smile and say "hello." Odds are, he'll at the very least say "hi" back, and you have the beginnings of a contact. If, however, he stops when he says "hi" back to you, be prepared to chat.

If you get involved in conversation with an important someone and the class session you were waiting for is starting, but the someone seems to have more time and appears to be interested in continuing the conversation, make a quick command decision about which is more important for your career: the personal contact or the class. If it's a class you really can't afford to miss, ask the speaker if the two of you could meet later for a cup of coffee at the speaker's convenience. If you choose to miss the class, ask if the speaker has time to go get a cup of coffee right now, or if he would like to find somewhere quiet to sit and chat. If the answer is "no," take it graciously, thank him for his time, and move on (maybe you can still make the class). If he says "yes," go for it.

11.3 *Between Classes, Be Where the People Are*

When you have a longer stretch between classes, take care of your bathroom run (to avoid interrupting a well-snagged contact), then plant yourself in whatever common areas are available. If the conference is in a hotel setting, one of the best places to meet speakers in a low-key situation (at least if you're of legal drinking age) is the bar. (And if you aren't old enough or aren't comfortable in the bar, find a seat close outside the entrance, and watch for opportunities.)

If you don't drink, don't worry about it. Virtually any full-service bar or lounge will have coffee, soft drinks, juice, or soda water available. (They'll often have the most comfortable chairs in the entire hotel, too.) And if you do drink, this isn't the time to do it anyway. For the contacts and conversations you're after, you absolutely must have a clear head. So wait to have that celebratory drink until you're back in your hotel room at the very end of the day. (Even then, keep in mind that you'll need that clear head tomorrow.)

Now, while you're sitting in the bar nursing your glass of cranberry juice and soda, if you see someone with a conference name tag sitting alone, ask if you can join that person and strike up a conversation. Even if he's "just" another attendee, this will give you a great chance to work your networking skills on each other. Use this opportunity to get a different slant on the conference experience and writing in general.

If the conference is being held at a college or other classroom setting, there's probably some sort of reception area or cafeteria where people hang out. Go there and do likewise, only instead of just killing time, use that time to increase your network of contacts. Try the old-faithful "hi" on a speaker who doesn't appear occupied, and gauge your next move by the speaker's response, just as you would in the hallway. Even if the only available speaker is a poet and your only interest is hard-line journalistic nonfiction, *no properly made networking contact is ever wasted.* That poet may well be the second cousin of an editor you've been dying to meet, or may just be a nice person you ought to know. At absolute minimum, you'll be practicing your networking skills for use on other speakers.

11.4 Keep Your Mind on Your Manners

If the speaker you've shanghaied happens to be in a field you don't think very highly of, don't you *dare* show any contempt. You must always assume that *any* speaker has paid her dues and is worthy of your respect; even if you have solid evidence to the contrary, being rude will only damage your reputation. And any writer, in any area of endeavor, can teach you something you didn't know, if you pay attention. Listen attentively, don't interrupt, ask intelligent questions, and be courteous.

The "no contempt" rule applies to your fellow attendees, too. The universe really isn't going to end if your current novel puts *War and Peace* to shame, and the man from Des Moines you just met over coffee writes for his local weekly shopper. You're both writers. Be civil, be friendly, and don't ever be a snob.

If you're polite and show the same interest in other people's writing that you expect them to show in yours, you might just learn something. Don't show contempt for your own writing or anyone else's. You're entitled to your opinions, but voicing them in public can plant your foot firmly (and often inextricably) in your mouth. Keep your negative value judgments to yourself. As human beings, and as writers, every person at that conference deserves your respect, yourself included.

So what should you do if the conversation you're joining in centers around bashing a writer? Simple. Don't play along. There's nothing wrong with having and voicing opinions, whether about one piece of writing or a whole category of writing, but that doesn't give anyone the right to bash the people who performed the writing. They still sweated over each and every page, just like you did with your magnum opus, and they're entitled to the same respect.

11.5 Recognize the Value of Local Contacts

Conferences are a great place to meet other writers from your local area or people who are writing in your field, as well as expanding your contacts outside your location and area of interest. (And if you've been searching for other writers to form a critique group, especially if the conference you're attending is close to home, ask the organizers if there's a bulletin board where you can post a notice.)

11.6 Make Creative Eavesdropping Your New Hobby

While you're roaming the hallways or common areas, keep your ears open. If a speaker is in close conversation with just one other person, follow your instincts as to whether you should join in. Watch for clues in the speaker's behavior. If she's staring intently into the attendee's eyes, if her voice is pitched low so that only the attendee can hear, if she's keeping her body language close and personal, you should probably stay out.

If, however, she's pausing frequently to look around the room, pitching her voice so that it carries beyond just the one person she's talking with, and her body language is relaxed and expansive, you're probably safe to stand within hearing range, nodding and smiling when you catch the speaker's eye. Wait for an opportunity when she acknowledges your presence and invites you into the conversation.

If a speaker is talking with several attendees (or a combination of other speakers and attendees), it should be safe for you to approach, using the same technique we suggested above: Stand within hearing range, nod and respond to what's being said, and watch for opportunities to gracefully insert yourself into the flow of conversation.

Occasionally, even a multiperson conversation will be private, so use some judgment in deciding whether to join in. You can always wait out of privacy range for the speaker to finish the conversation, then nab him as the party breaks up. As always, if you ask the speaker for a few minutes of his time and he says "no," thank him and let him walk away. A speaker who doesn't want to talk to you won't do your career any good. If you bow out gracefully and let him go, you may even get another chance with this person, if you handled yourself professionally and politely.

11.7   Secondhand Wisdom

You can learn a great deal from somebody else's question. You don't have to be the center of attention in a conversation to make a contact; laid-back participation will often gain you far more respect than hogging center stage. We've both learned any number of tricks of the trade by catching bits and pieces of other people's conversations in hallways, at banquet tables, and the like. If someone else asks a question that you've always wanted answered, listen attentively to the response. Add your own spin on the subject, if your instincts tell you to join in. The whirl of talk at a conference banquet table or buffet line is a great place to listen, learn, and respond without much fear of interrupting or crashing in on a private conversation.

11.8   Avoid the Commuting Blues

If the conference is in one location and your hotel is in another, don't waste your commuting time while you're riding on the shuttle. If some attendees are shuttling back and forth, it's a fair bet that some speakers are, too. Remember all your schmoozing techniques and watch for opportunities during that commute. At the very least, you should be able to strike up nodding acquaintances with the other attendees and speakers on the shuttle; at best, you may be able to plant networking seeds that could very well bloom while the conference is still going on.

Don't try to hold an actual business meeting on the bus; it's too good a way to get motion sick all over a speaker and yourself (or even the other way around)! But you can chat up that agent or editor you haven't been able to get close to, and ask if the two of you could get together later to visit. (If possible, make your appointment with the speaker for the same day; you're much less likely to forget or to be forgotten.)

All of the rest of the networking pointers apply, including remembering to say "thank you" both for the time spent visiting on the bus and for the later appointment, if any. If the answer to any of your requests is "no," thank him for his time and interest and move on. If you've asked, been turned down, and said "thank you," and there's still more trip to go, turn back to your notes or review the day's agenda.

The shuttle is also a great place to commiserate with your fellow attendees on sore feet, exhaustion, frustration, and the like. But be aware of the other ears sharing the bus with you. Don't allow yourself to get caught up in venting frustrations over a speaker while there are other speakers (or even other attendees you don't know) listening.

Bad form, bad manners, and bad business. If the attendee you're visiting with persists in complaining, disassociate yourself from the complainer as politely as possible, so you don't get slapped with the same bad manners label.

If the conference doesn't provide a shuttle, ask the speakers and other attendees if anyone would like to share a cab. This will cut your costs and give you an opportunity to schmooze one on one.

11.9 *Make Your Hearty Partying Pay*

Once the day's classes and workshops are finished, most of the conference participants will probably settle down for an evening of socializing. If there are a variety of parties available to attendees, choose which you'd like to attend by considering who's hosting the party, who's likely to be attending (guesswork, but you should be able to get some idea from who's hosting), and where the party is being held (it's easier to drop in on three or four parties in the same hotel than to go from one hotel to another).

If one or more of the parties is by invitation only, *don't try to crash it.* However, if you've made a strong contact with either a speaker or an attendee who has an invitation, and you believe this particular party could be important for you, (politely) ask the invited person if you might tag along. If the answer is "no," don't push it. There are certain to be other evening festivities you can get into without any trouble.

Once you're at a party, take stock of the situation. Is this a gathering of speakers only, attendees only, or a mixture? You'll probably make the best contacts in a mixed crowd setting, but you should be able to find some good networking fodder at either of the other types, too. If you don't see anyone you know, walk up to the nearest friendly face and say "hello." Repeat as necessary, until you find someone with whom you make at least a small click. Keep your business cards handy; stay polite, even in the face of base rudeness; and keep smiling.

Cruise the munchies table once in a while, but be careful not to overload your hands. (You'll need to be able to easily reach those business cards, won't you?) And remember to drink sensibly. You're still working the conference, and all the rules still apply.

Here's a situation that we've found ourselves in, and we're not alone here. You've just taken the last (enormous) bite of that delicious fudge brownie, turned your back in order to wolf down a mouthful, and realize you're looking straight into the eyes of the top agent on your hopefuls list.

What do you do? Well, if you're like most of us, you hold your napkin over your mouth while you blush and gulp madly away. Once the brownie is no longer in evidence, you smile sheepishly, shrug a bit, and say something like, "I'm a sucker for chocolate after a day like this. How 'bout you?" With any luck at all, the conversation will be off and running, and you'll even have something of a head start (provided your A list agent has a sense of humor—and if she doesn't, how has she survived in publishing?).

Set yourself a reasonable curfew that will allow you to cruise some of the parties, but to still get whatever amount of sleep you need to make the next day professionally productive.

11.10   School's Out

As the conference draws to a close, don't panic over contacts you haven't made. Focus instead on the contacts you *have* made, taking the time to catch up with each of them you can to say thanks, goodbye, and wish them a safe trip home. There will be other opportunities to connect with the people you missed, and a frenzied last-minute contact is as memorable as no contact at all.

The end of the conference will provide you with one more chance to offer rides to any speakers who have to get to the airport, so you'll have a bit more time to visit and schmooze with people. Be sure you know the flight schedules of any speakers you've committed to transport, so you can get them to the airport in plenty of time to make their flight. If you only give a ride to one speaker or one batch of speakers (or if this is your last speaker or group to transport), try to arrange your arrival at the airport to allow for one last cup of coffee together in the airport restaurant or lounge.

At a conference several years ago, we cemented our contact with a publisher we'd been escorting by getting him to the airport in plenty of time for his flight back home. He appreciated not having to race for his plane, and the three of us had time to sit and visit over tea in the coffee shop. Two years later, he published a short story collection of ours. Because of the professional yet personable way we handled ourselves, he was predisposed in our favor; once he found he liked our writing, he offered us a contract.

Some conferences have an after-the-conference party or event, primarily for the volunteers and staffers, but sometimes open to other attendees. If you know of such a function (sometimes referred to as the "dodo party"), ask the organizers if you can drop in.

If you've been as helpful as we've suggested, and kept your cool when others around you have blown theirs, they'll be glad to have you. While you're unlikely to run across any speakers at this gathering, you'll be able to network with other writers in the conference area.

Contacts are contacts, and you can always use more connections in the writing field, whether they're pros or eager amateurs. Just be sure to leave yourself enough time and energy to get home safely.

12

Personal Consultations

PERSONAL CONSULTATIONS are one-on-one meetings between attendees and the agent or editor of their choice. These meetings are made available by the conference organizers either for a fee or as a part of the registration and last about fifteen to twenty minutes. We don't ordinarily recommend these sessions, preferring the more personal contacts available through networking. But if you *do* sign up for a personal consultation, here are some tips to follow to get the most out of that meeting.

12.1 More Homework

Once you know with whom you'll be meeting (and if you haven't received confirmation of that person's identity in advance of the conference, call the organizers and *ask*), start doing your homework. Remember the research we had you do in 6.1–6.6 regarding the contacts you hoped to make at the conference? Well, this time you need to be even more prepared, since you're going to be operating under a strict time limit and you'll be just one of probably several dozen writers having consultations with this one agent or editor. The last thing you'll want is to be remembered as the worst prepared writer he met with!

Using the resources recommended in chapter 6 and the Bibliography, do another layer of research on your consultation date. Read everything you can find about this person, using the market listings, the industry-specific magazines (also listed in chapter 6 and the Bibliography), newspapers, any source you can track down. Ask other writers you know about this person and his or her track record.

Do as much research as you reasonably have time for (and not at the expense of your other preconference work—after all, this is only one person out of many you're going to meet), until you have a pretty good mental picture of the agent or editor you're meeting with.

12.2 Don't Waste Your Time—Or Theirs

You need to decide what you're going to talk about. This is one situation where keeping your lip zipped won't do you any good, at least not until you've asked a question and are waiting for the answer, since the agent or editor hasn't any idea what you need to talk about or what you need. It's up to you to set the process in motion.

First, decide *exactly* what information you want to come away with. If your meeting is with an agent, is your goal to have this agent represent you? If that's the case, is your book-length writing at a stage where an agent could actually sell it? If not, all is not lost. If you're interested in being represented by this agent, but don't have any book projects at a marketable stage, take a sample of your best book project and polish it the very best you can. (If at all possible, put together a submission packet as explained in 8.3.) You may be able to lay the groundwork that will eventually put your writing into this agent's hands for marketing.

If your meeting is with an editor, is your goal to sell your manuscript to this editor? If this is the case, do you have a finished piece of writing that's suitable for this editor's area of expertise? If so, take that piece of writing and polish it to the best form you're capable of (and, if it's a book manuscript, prepare the rest of the submission packet, as discussed in 8.3).

Next, write down *every single question* you can imagine asking this agent or editor. Brainstorm on the subject over several days if you have to. Ask a writer friend to look over your list and suggest any questions you're missing.

Once you have this list on paper, go through it one question at a time. Cross off every redundancy and question you can answer yourself by doing some research. Compare your list to our collection of questions not to ask in chapter 7, and cross out any that fall into that category. Highlight every question that pertains to the agent's or editor's specific views, opinions, or personal preferences, since you probably won't be able to get those answers anywhere except from that person.

Now go back through your edited list and look *very* closely at the remaining questions. Break any compound questions into single components, so you'll be able to get more easily understood answers (and you'll be able to be sure which answer goes with which part of the question). You'll probably find some more questions that are so closely related that you can either just ask once, or modify one question to get multiple-question information.

At this point, you should have a list of no more than ten questions. Now look for the natural order of the questions you have left. In most cases, you should be able to identify a progression among the questions, but there's one in particular that should always be your last: Would you be interested in looking at this piece of my writing? You'll want to stay flexible on the timing of this, since some agents or editors will want to get this issue out of the way early on. Ideally, you should talk about your credentials first, then discuss the piece of writing you'd like to submit. But it's also possible that you will have handled your side of the conversation so well that the agent or editor asks you if she could see some of your writing. This really can happen, but you can't count on it; so be prepared to lead the way (see 12.5).

Now, hone your list down to the five or six absolutely most important questions. Be prepared to ask only as many questions as you estimate can be reasonably answered in the amount of time allotted (and since most of your questions won't have yes or no answers, figure at least two to three minutes per answer). Copy these questions onto your conference note pad, writing (or typing) them clearly and legibly so you aren't stuck trying to decipher your own handwriting on a tight timeline under nervous circumstances. Leave room between questions for your notes on the answers, since this makes it easier to decipher later. To overcome any nervousness at the session, practice your question-asking technique in front of a mirror or, better yet, with a writer friend, until you can clearly and simply state your questions.

Be sure to dress for comfort and professionalism, not flash. This is not a fashion show. You are making a professional contact, having your questions answered, and talking about your writing. Remember to wear a watch that keeps accurate time, because it's your responsibility to be aware of time limitations. The person in charge of the consultations will also be keeping track of time, but you shouldn't have to be told your time is up. This is just another point of professionalism and courtesy. (And *please* don't take off the watch and sit it in front of you; this makes you look too much like a state examiner timing a test, and doesn't exactly make for relaxed conversation. Just wear the watch on your wrist where you can casually check it throughout the session.)

12.3 Punctuality Counts

When the time arrives for your scheduled consultation, be sure *you* arrive on time. Being early won't hurt, as long as you remember to be patient and wait your turn. If the consultation before yours runs a few minutes over time, take it in stride. But if the session immediately prior to yours is running over by a half-hour or more, and there's no note or other indication that the whole schedule has been moved back, find the conference organizer or volunteer in charge of the sessions and ask him to interrupt the session. If there isn't a volunteer overseeing the consultations (and there should be at least one), locate another conference volunteer and ask her to let the agent or editor know that the writer's time is up.

If at all possible, do not interrupt someone else's session yourself to tell them time's up. It's not rude if a conference volunteer does it; it's part of her job. It could all too easily be construed as rude if you do it, so don't unless there's no other choice. However, no matter that they're running over time, it will still be interrupting the agent or editor in the midst of doing business, so don't force an interruption unless it's unavoidable.

Once your consultation time has come and the agent or editor is no longer occupied with another writer, walk in with your head up. Introduce yourself, shake hands, thank him or her for taking the time to meet with you, and sit down smiling. Set aside any aggravations you've had over delays or other conference problems; they don't belong in this room. Neither do any other aspects of bad mood or bad day. Leave all complaints at the door, and walk in with a fresh attitude.

You have every right to get your full time, even if you get a late start (so long as the late start wasn't caused by your tardiness; if it was, just make the best of it and ask your most important questions first). If earlier scheduling problems have thrown the agent's or editor's timeline out of whack (which often happens) and your session is cancelled (somewhat less common), keep your cool and ask when you can reschedule your session, maybe even over a cup of coffee at a later time. If you play it right, your courtesy and understanding could well turn your abbreviated consultation into a personal meeting and a much more memorable contact for both of you.

12.4 Make It Personal

Take a moment or two and ask this agent or editor how he's enjoying the conference. If he's from out of town, ask if he's ever been to wherever you are, or some other personable chitchat to humanize the situation. If he's acting impatient and anxious to get on with your questions, follow his lead and get down to business. If, however, he seems willing to chat for a moment, use it to your advantage. This moment of relaxation will help make you a real person in his mind, instead of just another name on a sheet of paper. Just be sure to not get too far off the subject at hand; you haven't enough time to wander very far afield, so wait for a break to gently bring the conversation back around to the reason you're both there.

Once the conversation turns back to business, pull out your list of questions and your (two) working pens. Ask your first question, looking him in the eye as often as possible and smiling when appropriate. Speak clearly and succinctly, with as few "uhs," "ahs," "ums," and "you knows" as possible. If the agent or editor asks you for clarification of a question, don't get flustered. Sometimes people need to know for sure what information you're seeking. Just reword or expand on your question until he has a better idea of what you're asking.

As your questions are answered, take accurate notes. But don't let your note taking get in the way of making frequent eye contact and verbal acknowledgments.

12.5   *Offering Your Work*

By the time you've reached that last, important question—"Would you be interested in seeing my work?"—the agent or editor should have a fairly good idea of who you are and what stage your writing has reached. (As a matter of fact, many agents and editors pride themselves on being able to tell whether someone can write, or has the potential to be a good writer, by the time they've talked with that individual for five minutes. Once again, it's a matter of professional attitudes and behavior paying off. And they're usually right.)

Have your high concept for the project ready for answering the inevitable "What's your story about?" If you've impressed him with your professionalism and your preparation for this meeting, and *if* your project is in an area of writing that he handles, and *if* he feels, from meeting with you, that your writing (and your attitude) should be marketable or close to it, and *if* he thinks he has a fair chance of selling this project, based on your high concept and his estimation of you and your potential, he may then say, "Yes, send me your work and I'll take a look."

If any one or more of these "ifs" isn't there, he probably won't give you permission to send the project. As you can see from the whole series of "ifs" involved, not getting permission to submit doesn't mean you're a bad writer or a bad person. As we have discussed throughout this book, there are myriad reasons why he may say "no," so do your best to not take it as a personal rejection. It's not, and taking it personally will just set you back.

So what do you do if you get a "no"? Thank him again for taking the time to meet with you and answer your questions, wish him a great time over the balance of the conference and a safe trip home, and exit gracefully. You've still gotten answers to your questions, which will help you in other parts of the business. Besides, there are more people for you to contact, so you really have no reason to be upset. You're not going to succeed with everyone you meet at the conference. And what would you do with fifteen agents, anyway? No matter how his side of the meeting went, even if he was less than totally polite to you, don't badmouth him and don't carry a grudge. This is a big business but a small world, and you can't afford to hold bad feelings against someone who might help you five, ten, or even fifteen years down the line.

Do not under any circumstances send your work to someone who has said "no"! It's rude and it makes you look bad.

In the event of a "yes," the first thing you do is say "thank you." (See 9.6 for more details on this process.) Ask, too, if he'd prefer the full manuscript (unlikely, if it's book-length) or an appropriate submission packet (as described in 8.3). Whatever he says he wants is exactly what you should send—no exceptions. Don't blow a well-made contact by not following instructions (we've seen it happen all too often).

After you've verified all the mailing information, give him your best (and most honest) estimation of how soon you'll be mailing the package. If he asks you to wait a few weeks to send it, abide by his wishes.

If an editor says, "Yes, send it to me and I'll take a look," does that mean you've made a sale? *No!* Once again, all you've earned is an opportunity to bypass the slush pile.

If an agent has said, "Yes, I'll look at your work," does that mean he's now representing you? *No!* All a "yes" answer to that question means is that you now have an opportunity to jump past the slush pile.

In either case, be sure your cover letter mentions the timing and circumstances of your meeting, and mentions that he said you could send him your work.

Don't underestimate the value of these opportunities. Handled properly, a personal consultation can be as valuable to your career as a well-timed schmooze.

12.6 *Ending Your Consultation*

As you reach a point two or three minutes from the end of the scheduled time, gather up your materials and thank him for taking the time to meet with you. This way, you won't be rushed as the consultation ends, and you'll look much more professional and in control.

If your conversation is going so well that you feel it should continue, ask if he would consider meeting with you at another time (or immediately following the consultation, if he has the time), in a less formal setting, to continue chatting. If he agrees to or suggests a continuation, thank him and ask him when or where (getting an exact time and location, if at all possible). Use your best schmoozing techniques during the continued visit. Whether or not he agrees to look at your work, you may have just begun a strong professional relationship.

If the questions you asked led the two of you down too many side roads or he's been a bit long-winded in his answers, in either case leaving you with questions unanswered and no time left, ask him if you could write to him after the conference, in order to get answers to the rest of your questions. If he says "no," thank him and move on. In all probability, you'll find someone else at the conference who can answer them. If he says "yes," thank him and follow the procedures in 9.6. Then follow up with a letter setting forth your remaining questions and reminding him of the circumstances of the consultation and your earlier meeting, just as you would in sending your manuscript (we'll give you specific how-tos in 13.4). And if he said "yes" to more questions but "no" to looking at your work, *don't* send him the materials anyway.

As soon after the consultation as practical, sit down with your questions and flesh out your notes on his answers while your recollection is still fresh. If more questions occurred to you as a result of some of his answers, jot them down so you can ask the next person you schmooze. Catch your breath for a moment, then dive back in. You've still got more conference to work!

Part Three

After the Conference

13

Once You're Home

THE CONFERENCE IS OVER and you're on your way home. What can you do to make sure you get the most value from all those contacts you made and all the work you've done?

13.1 First Things First: Take Care of You

Your first task after a conference is to give yourself a chance to recover. Unpack and get settled back in. Treat yourself to a long bath or some time in a hot tub or sauna—something to help you relax and unwind after a strenuous working conference. Spend a few hours doing whatever relaxes you the most, but avoid activities that may cloud your recollection of the conference (which usually precludes heavy drinking or other recreational chemicals). Your goal is to relax your body while leaving your mind functioning.

If you have any last-minute thoughts that you fear may not hold on until morning, jot them down, but don't spend too much time. Remember, right now your primary task is to rest and relax so that you'll be ready to take the next steps. Get a good night's sleep (especially if you have to jump right back into the workaday world—and why didn't you listen to us and schedule that extra day to rest?). Plan on tackling your follow-up work as soon as possible.

13.2 Cement Your Contacts

The day after the conference is over, when you're rested, alert, and ready to go, organize your business cards and notes on schmoozing contacts with speakers and other writers, filling in any blanks in your recollection. Sort your information on your various contacts as follows.

13.2.1 Speakers with Whom You Made a Schmoozing Connection, but Who Didn't Agree to Look at Your Work or to Answer Questions

Write thank you notes to each speaker in this group (see our suggestions for proper stationery in 13.3). Mention the details of your meeting with that speaker, tell her how much you appreciated her taking the time to talk with you, and thank her for her interest. If you know she's going to attend a conference that you're planning on attending later, say so, and tell her you're looking forward to seeing her there. It doesn't hurt to wish her luck on whatever current project of hers the two of you may have discussed (or you may have heard about at the conference). Good wishes are nice for anyone to hear, whatever the listener's professional status. Try to keep your note fairly brief, thereby acknowledging how busy the speaker is and how much you appreciate the time she took to visit with you.

13.2.2 Other Attendees With Whom You Made a Networking Contact

Write the same sort of thank you notes to the members of this group (and note the suggestions in 13.3). It's nearly as important for you to connect with other still-struggling writers as with the pros, so your notes to other attendees should be as heartfelt and pleasant as the ones you write to speakers. They don't, however, necessarily need to be as long. A simple "it was great to meet you; good luck in your career; hope we can get together again sometime" will work just fine.

Once these two groups of notes are written, mail them right away. They won't do you any good whatsoever sitting on your desk, and they should be in the mail toward their destinations by no later than a week after the end of the conference. Much longer than that and you might as well not bother. If you allow too much time to pass before these people receive your note, it's all too probable they'll no longer remember you at all.

13.2.3 Speakers Who've Agreed to Look at Your Work

For these speakers, you need to do a bit more than mail a thank you note. First, prepare a cover letter (see 13.3 for suggestions on paper), mentioning the circumstances of your meeting with them and any other details that you think will boost their memory of you. You should also state that you asked for and received their permission to submit to them, since they may not remember the names of everyone they said could send them work. A brief physical description of yourself ("the short woman with red hair wearing a purple blazer," etc.) won't hurt either, to better help them remember you. You should both open and close your letter by thanking them for taking the time to meet with you and for agreeing to look at your manuscript. (These people have agreed to do you both a personal and a professional favor, and there's nothing in the world wrong with acknowledging that fact.)

Next, go over your work and ask yourself these questions:

- *Is it absolutely clean and error-free?* (Ask a writer friend to proofread if necessary.)
- *Is the writing as taut and active as I can make it?*
- *Is it the best writing I can do, at this time?*
- *Is it fully detailed but succinct, and as full of the passion of the book as I can make it?*
- *Does it include sufficient information to give the reader a feel for the completed work?*
- *Do all of its parts follow proper formatting, as detailed in 8.3?*
- *Have I included a SASE for the agent's or editor's response?*

Add the cover letter and mail this puppy out; it won't make you a nickel sitting on your desk.

13.2.4 Speakers Who've Agreed to Answer Your Written Questions

We've left this group for last, because these are, in some ways, the least urgent of your follow-up mailings. You can either prepare a separate cover letter to go with your typed list of questions, or combine the two into a single piece. In either case, the letter portion should include the same pieces as your cover letters to the group in 13.2.3, on the same type of paper (see 13.3). You should mention the circumstances of your meeting with the speaker and other memory-boosting details. State that he gave you permission to submit your unanswered questions. And, as always, open and close your letter by thanking him for taking the time to meet with you and agreeing to answer your remaining questions.

Whether you've included your questions in the letter or typed them separately, be sure that at least your last name and a page number is on every piece of paper you send, in case your packet gets shuffled with the other fifteen (or fifty) on the speaker's desk. Your questions should be clearly (*not defensively*) stated. Leave room for the speaker's answers. Keep your questions concise and limited in number (no more than ten, at the very outside, to any one speaker). Be sure to include a large enough SASE for the speaker to return the answers.

13.3 The Right Stationery for the Best Impression

Let's talk notes and note papers for a moment. The notes that you're writing to the groups listed in 13.2.1 and 13.2.2 can be on letterhead or printed out on computer paper, although that doesn't give quite the same personal feeling (and they should *never* be an obvious form letter). You can also use note paper or note cards and handwrite your message, so long as you remember one primary point: These notes are strengthening your *professional* contacts, so the kitten-with-ball-of-yarn or puppies-in-a-basket cards are out. If you want to use note cards or note paper, find a design that suits your professional personality, whatever that might be.

Our preference for these groups is to send handwritten notes on Oregon scenic note cards; the Oregon photographs or sketches remind the recipient of the beauty of our home state, and the contents let them know we cared enough to take the time to write them a personal note. Even though Lee's arthritis makes writing by hand very painful (and Steve's handwriting isn't exactly the most legible in the world), we still make the effort. After all, these contacts were worth spending our limited conference time to make; they should be worth taking the extra effort to cement the memory in the speaker's mind. (We send these notes even if we were also speakers at the conference; these people are still important professional contacts, and we still follow up.)

As for the cover letters to the groups in 13.2.3 and 13.2.4, these should be typed or computer printed in standard business letter format, on either your letterhead, or blank white paper. No note cards this time, especially for the group in 13.2.3, since this is a formal submission letter.

13.4 Rating the Conference

Now that the notes, work, and questions have been mailed, it is time to sit down and honestly evaluate how well you did at the conference, and how well the conference did for you. Sit somewhere comfortable, either in front of your computer or a pad of paper, with limited distractions and with your conference notes and the agenda close at hand. Writing down your reasons for your evaluations of each category, and your ideas for changes, consider the following:

13.4.1 Workshops

- *Which workshop sessions do you feel were the most successful for you?* Why did these sessions work better than the others you attended? How much of your feeling of success is connected to the teacher? The subject? The setting? The other writers attending? Questions asked by your fellow students? Were there any parts of the otherwise successful workshops that could have been better for you? Could the subject matter have been slanted more effectively for your needs?
- *Which workshops were the least successful for you?* What didn't work about these sessions? Would you have enjoyed the workshop better if it had been taught by someone else? Were there too few questions, or too many? Was the timing of the session off (either too early or too late in the day, in competition with too many other important classes)? Would you have liked the session better if the slant had been different? Was the room uncomfortable, or overcrowded? Was the sound system adequate? Did you feel the other writers attending the workshop were satisfied? Were there any aspects of the unsuccessful workshops that you *did* like?

- *What could you have done to make the workshops more successful?* Were you unprepared for the session? Was it a case of a satisfactory workshop that was inappropriate to your needs? If you were running the conference, how would you change those workshops to make them more successful for a writer like you?

13.4.2 Speakers

- *Which speakers were the most helpful for you?* Why do these particular speakers stand out in your memory? Did you get the most help from them in a workshop setting, or by schmoozing? Which speakers did you click with professionally, and which do you think will "just" become friends? Do you feel you'll eventually make money based on your contact with these speakers? Which speakers were the best for your ego, whether or not they'll be of help in the future? (A willingness to encourage new writers is a sign of a generous spirit, always an invaluable personality trait.)

  You should also note the occupations of the various speakers with whom you made good contacts. While making strong contacts with a bunch of agents is definitely a good thing, connecting with editors and publishers will probably have greater benefits for your billfold in the long run. You can really only have one agent at a time, but you can work with lots of editors and publishers at the same time.

- *Which speakers were the least helpful to you?* Why didn't you click with these speakers? Did you have a personality clash with any of them? (These are sometimes unavoidable, so don't feel bad, so long as you didn't do anything to cause or exacerbate the conflict.) Did you catch some of these speakers at a bad time? Do you feel that any of them were set against you before you opened your mouth? (Personal prejudices do exist.)

- *What could you have done to improve your contact with these speakers?* You can't be responsible for someone else's bad mood (or bad behavior), but you may have played a part in the contact either not happening or going sour. Replay your encounters with those speakers in your mind. Given another opportunity, what would *you* have done differently? Is there a chance you could make a good contact with any of those speakers when you run into them again? Was the contact so negative that you shouldn't attempt to repair the damage later? Even in the most unfortunate of bad connections, your job remains the same: Stay professional. It doesn't matter what your personal feelings are; when you run across someone with whom you have bad history, remain polite and discrete. Don't tell tales, and don't hold grudges. (Besides, by making sure you stay professional, no matter what happens, you win!)

13.4.3 Other Conference Events

- *Which nonworkshop events were the most successful for you?* This category includes opening ceremonies, banquets (whether breakfast, lunch, or dinner), parties, closing ceremonies—you get the picture. While these events are secondary in importance to the workshops you paid to attend, they still provided networking opportunities that you (hopefully) took advantage of. Which of these events really paid off for you? How much of that success was due to your own efforts? As you list the various informal events that worked for you, note which speakers and contacts you made at which events, both by name and by occupation. (This will help you plan your time at your next writer's conference.)
- *Which nonworkshop events were the least successful?* How much of this lesser value was due to your efforts, or lack thereof? You may well find that there are some events that you just won't bother with at the next conference you attend, since your time and energy will be limited and you can't really afford to waste either one. For instance, we rarely bother anymore with banquets. In our conference experience, the food is frequently awful and nearly always grossly overpriced; the service is often atrocious; and the circumstances limit the networking opportunities. However, prebanquet cocktail parties or receptions are nearly always on our itinerary, since we can usually control what we have to pay for (and since we don't drink, we don't have to spend much). The less formal circumstances make for much better schmoozing. We just usually disappear before the banquet starts.
- *What could you have done to make these events more successful and useful for your career?* While one person can only do so much to affect the end results, make notes of any ideas you have for either

improving the events themselves, or at least improving your participation in them. Were there any events that you think should have been included, but weren't? Were there conference attendees who should have been included in some events, but weren't? (And can you figure out why they weren't?) Were attendees included in some events when you feel they really shouldn't have been?

13.4.4 Homework

- *What homework could you have done better?* Did your homework turn up any information that proved faulty? Did you make erroneous assumptions based on any of your research? Could you have organized your notes in a more effective way (or left out some information that proved extraneous)?
- *What homework should you have done, but didn't?* Were there any gaps in your research that left you flat-footed? Were there speakers at the conference whom you should have researched, but didn't (excluding last-minute additions not announced in the registration materials; there's nothing you can do about those)? Why not? Were there errors in your research criteria? Are there market listings you should have referred to, but didn't? Why?
- *What homework should you do for the next conference you attend?* Now that you've finished this conference, you may find gaps in the research you performed that you can fill in for your next conference experience. Note any additional branches or sources of research material for use in your next conference preparation.

13.4.5 Other Attendees

- *Were the other writers in attendance as serious about their craft as you expected?* There's no reason you can't be serious about writing and have fun, too. But did you think the majority of the other attendees took their writing seriously? Too seriously? Did you get the feeling the other attendees were as professional as you were? How did their behavior differ from yours? Was this conference a good choice for your level of writing and experience? How would you describe the "typical" attendee of this conference? How did this typical attendee match up to your expectations, based on the conference literature and your research?

- *Were the other attendees as experienced in their craft as you expected?* How did their experience level match up with yours? Did you feel their behavior was comparable to their experience level? Acting more professional than your actual writing credits is exactly what we're trying to teach you to do—but what about writers with lots of credits but unprofessional behavior?
- *Were the other attendees as prepared as you expected?* Did you get the feeling the other attendees just showed up, with no preparation? Or did you feel they were blasé professionals who'd been through this a hundred times, while you were going through your first time? It's okay to be more prepared than the people around you; that just gives you an extra leg-up. However, it can be annoying to be surrounded by amateurs who are acting like amateurs (or worse, professionals acting like amateurs), while you're doing your best to act like a pro. While this makes your professional behavior stand out in contrast, it can still make for an unpleasant conference.
- *Were the other attendees interested in the same types of writing as you are?* This isn't an essential aspect, since character, plot, editing, sales, and the like are subjects that interest writers across the board. In the early days, long before Kevin Costner and *Dances with Wolves*, we were frequently the only writers at a conference who would admit to writing westerns. While various genre have their own specialized conferences, you can learn a lot from writers with different interests, too. If the majority of attendees write in the same field or genre as you, did you find this helpful? If the majority write in different genre, did you find that difference helpful? How did their similarity or dissimilarity of interest affect your overall conference experience? Would that (dis)similarity change your choice of the next conference you attend? Why?

13.5 How Did You Do?

The purpose of this review process is to evaluate the conference you've just attended and to project how you'll do at your next conference. Review your answers to the questions stated above, and consider how they will affect your next conference. Will you choose a different conference, because of how you did at this one? How would you have changed this conference and your performance, had you the power to travel back in time?

Congratulations! You've just completed the first stage of the homework for your next writer's conference. How's it feel?

14

Where Do You Go from Here?

YOU'VE RETURNED HOME, rested, and written and mailed your follow-up notes and packages. If you're a day-jobber, you're probably back to work, and the outside world is clamoring for your attention. Before you give yourself over entirely to the "real world," what should you do to retain the most value from the conference just finished, in preparation for your next conference attack?

14.1 Focus on Your New Information

Before you file them away for the future, review your conference notes (and your postconference evaluation) for new ideas, new information, and new possibilities gleaned from your conference classes. File in your memory any pointers you can use in marketing your writing (new markets, new angles, new ways to better focus your marketing, new needs for older markets). Note in your market listings any editorial changes or major changes in market needs that you learned of at the conference. Remind yourself of any attitude changes suggested at the conference, since you're unlikely to adopt the new attitudes into your behavior without some effort.

If your notes contain any gems dropped by conference speakers, post the most encouraging statements in your office or writing area where you will see them often—preferably every time you sit down to write. (One wall in our office is covered with acceptance letters, award certificates, and encouraging notes we've received over the years from editors, teachers, students, and contests.) It's a good idea to post at least one new thing after each conference you attend; the new sign will act as a reminder of the work you did and what you accomplished. If you've come up with nothing better, feel free to use our suggestion from chapter 1: A WRITER IS SOMEONE WHO WRITES. Print this in large, bold type and stick it to a wall where you can't help but see it every time you sit down to write. Trust us: There will be days that this is the only thing that will keep you going; take your encouragement from wherever you can find it.

Look over the submission plan you had for your writing before the conference. You should now have ideas on how to improve both your writing and the focus of your submissions to greatly increase your chance of sales. You should also have more information regarding contests you should be entering, whether because of direct information provided at the conference or your own ideas inspired by that information. What should you change, based on what you've learned? Have you missed out on sales because you were submitting to the wrong markets? Were you submitting to the right markets, but with the wrong manuscripts? Are there pieces missing from your submission packet? Between the research we've had you doing and what you've learned at the conference, you may want to totally revamp your marketing plan (and if you didn't have a marketing plan before the conference, you need one now). By marketing plan, we mean both your plan for placing each manuscript *and* your plans for your writing career overall.

Reviewing your career market plan should include one more trip back through your market listings. This time, look specifically for markets that you didn't think you could write for, or weren't within your reach (for whatever reason), before the conference. There may be an entire branch of magazine or book publishers that you've never considered writing for, simply because you didn't think your writing fit (whether by subject matter or quality), which you now realize are available to you. Highlight these "new" markets, since they've never seen your work before. You and your writing may be exactly what they've been looking everywhere for.

14.2 Apply What You've Learned

Once you've reviewed your notes, sit down and draw up a new marketing plan for your career. As the groundwork for that plan, sort through your writing and pull out pieces of your work that you believe are marketable *now*. Go through and read each piece, and objectively evaluate the writing: Is this piece really marketable, or should it be reedited and improved on? Once you have a collection of work that you believe (after careful consideration) to be marketable in its current condition, list the title of each manuscript or project on a separate piece of paper. Write down the markets that have already seen and rejected the work, with any notes or comments you received from the editor.

Now, with your current market listings in hand, come up with another five markets that you think (based on your new information from the conference) would be interested in that work. Be sure to go through your "new" markets, and add as many from that collection as is suitable. One note: Under most circumstances, don't send more than one piece or project to the same market at the same time (and *never* more than one in an envelope, under any circumstances). After all, it's hard enough to compete with all the other writers out there. Why compete with yourself, too? A few of the science fiction/fantasy magazines are exceptions to this rule, but it all depends on the editor. If you heard an editor at the conference say this was okay with her, then go ahead. Otherwise, one piece at a time to a magazine or publisher is a good idea.

Prepare each piece as a complete package (remember the guidelines in 8.3) and send it to the first market on its list. Write down the date you send the packet out, the date you should expect a response (based on the response time stated in the market listing), and the date (usually a month after the expected response date) when you should send a polite, low-key follow-up letter, if you haven't heard from the editor yet. As the rejections come in (and we *all* get rejections, no matter how many sales we have under our proverbial belts), write down the date you received the rejection, together with any comments you got from the editor. Then prepare a new packet and get it out the door to the next market on the list, within twenty-four hours if at all possible. As we've said before, that writing isn't going to make you any money sitting on your desk.

14.3 Deal with Rejection from Conference Contacts

Speaking of rejections, what if one of the people you wrote to in 13.2.3 rejects your work? No matter how strong a contact you've made, the work you submitted may not be right for that agent or editor for business reasons. Try not to take this any more personally than any other rejection. The best statement of attitude on rejection that we've ever heard comes from Barbara Kingsolver: "Consider that you've addressed [your submission], 'To the editor who can appreciate my work,' and it has simply come back stamped 'Not at this address.'" You have, at a minimum, accomplished something you may never have done before: Your work reached past the slush pile and was considered seriously.

If the agent or editor rejected your work, but suggested another editor or agency that might be interested, follow up on that suggestion. In your letter with the new version of the packet, mention the recommendation of the first editor or agent by name, and get this new packet out the door as soon as possible.

What if one of speakers to whom you either submitted a packet or sent a list of questions fails to respond at all? In the case of a submission packet, allow at least a month more than the response time stated for that speaker in the market listings. If you still haven't heard, send a brief, polite letter, asking if the work is still under consideration, and enclosing a SASE for their response. If you haven't received answers to your list of questions after six months, send the same type of short, low-key letter and a SASE.

14.4 Get Back to Your Writing

Now that all your primary postconference assimilation work is done, forget about it. Yes, you read us correctly. Clear your conscious mind of all the marketing techniques, writing tips, and networking contacts you made at the conference. Your subconscious will manage this information for you just fine, and you don't want to be stumbling over lumps of data when you're trying to write. Trust your subconscious to process the information and feed it into the flow of your creative mind when it's needed—and not before.

Sit down at your desk and write. Even if you were in the midst of a major project before you left for the conference, take a short break and start something new. Begin a new piece (we find short stories work great for this purpose), ideally something in a genre or form you've never written before. The point is, look at writing in general and your writing in specific with fresh eyes. Your conference experience can change your writing in many positive ways, *if* you're open to the changes involved. This is part of why we suggest taking time out from your major project to write something short, preferably something new and completely different from anything else you've done before. Your big project will be there when you get back to it, and your writing will be better for the break. There are as many angles on writing as there are writers, and this is your chance to come at your writing from a direction you've never before considered. This is also a way to let the break you took from writing to attend the conference, and the conference experience itself, boost your writing onto a new plateau.

If you've never before seen your writing go into a growth spurt, this may come as something of a shock. However, we can vouch for the probability of this change, since every single time we've taken any kind of substantial break from writing, whether to attend a conference or to deal with some outside world trauma, when we returned to the computer, our writing has leapt to an entirely new level. And yes, this can be a pain when you're in the middle of a novel and the new writing is vastly superior to the old, but that's what rewrites are for.

You'll have new eyes and new energy to apply to your writing; don't waste either one by insisting that your writing continue on its preconference path. Yes, this can be frightening, especially if you've been writing the same way and in the same genre for years.

Growth is change, and change is often very uncomfortable. Maybe the reason your writing hasn't sold (or hasn't sold as much as you'd like) is locked into your old methods, and you'll have to unlock your internal doors before you can change—and improve—your writing. Open yourself to the possibilities of new directions and new writing, and you may well find the sales you've wished for along the way.

14.5 Pat Yourself on the Back—You've "Done Good"!

Your eyes are open, your mind is clear, and there's a blank page in front of you. Go for it! You've done all the work, now reap the rewards. You've earned them!

15

Other Networking Opportunities

As we mentioned at the beginning of this book, networking is not something you go to one particular place, such as a writer's conference, to do. It is a twenty-four-hours-a-day, seven-days-a-week, fifty-two-weeks-a-year job.

We've used writer's conferences to teach you the basics of networking, simply because writer's conferences are the largest, most prominent example of networking opportunities in the writer's world. But a writer's conference is, by no stretch of the imagination, the *only* opportunity for networking.

15.1 The Incomplete List

There are many, many other opportunities out there just waiting for you. This is by no means a complete list. All we're trying to do is open your eyes to the availability of a vast number of contacts you might not think of on your own, to teach you how to recognize these opportunities when (or even better, before) they appear.

There is no specific order of importance to this list. Taking advantage of any one of these opportunities may turn out to be the best move you've ever made in your career. Or, it may make no difference whatsoever. There's no way to tell how it will work out until the present wends its way into the path of history.

15.1.1 Readings and Signings

Watch your local paper for listings of upcoming readings or signings by authors whose work you admire; or authors who have written a book or books something like yours; or authors who have been published by a publisher you feel is just right for your book; or authors who are located in your hometown. Get on the mailing lists of bookstores in your area, so you have the fastest possible information for your calendar.

It doesn't matter where the writer came from. A local writer who has just had her book published may have as much clout as a writer from the opposite end of the country, at least where the publisher is concerned. Every famous (and not-so-famous) writer must live some-where.

What does matter, though, is the web of connections this writer may have at her disposal and her willingness to share that information. The former can be investigated by a little homework, such as a visit to *Books in Print* at your local library or bookseller. As to the latter, well, you pays your money and you takes your chances.

Does this sound cold-blooded?

In a way, it is. In another way, it is just running *potential* informa-tion and contacts through the screens of applicability.

If the author makes it through your screen setup intact, then you need to make a point of being there for her reading. If she doesn't, then your attendance is optional. (But remember, no contact is wast-ed, even if you're "just" meeting another writer.)

If you decide to go, get there a little early. Often, there's enough time before the reading begins that you can make your initial contact. Take advantage of your opportunity, and strike up a conversation. (See 10.9 for information on making contacts.)

15.1.2 Writer's Groups

Not all writer's groups are worthy of the name, and there's a strong difference of opinion in the writing community as to their value. Some people believe that a writer's group is a complete waste of time, energy, and money (membership fees) that could be better spent on writing and writing expenses. We believe that, especially in the early stages of a writer's career, membership and participation in a writer's group can put a writer in touch with the industry like no other entity.

Before you decide to go out and join the nearest writer's group, check out what's available. If you live in or near a city, you probably have a number to choose from, both genre-specific and general membership. Go to a meeting or two. Find out if these are people who are actively pursuing a professional career, or just happen to like being around "real writers." Find out what kind and quality of people the group brings in as speakers, and what services the organization offers.

If, after consideration and questions, a particular writer's group looks like a fit for you, join it. Even more important, *get involved* with the group. Volunteer in areas where you can help make it a better group, and in areas where it can help your career more directly—such as providing transportation for visiting speakers.

Aside from that, follow your nose to better contacts—professional writers in the group, or sponsors, or advisers, or . . .

15.1.3 Booksellers

Bookstore owners and clerks, or publishers' sales reps who visit the stores to sell their wares, hold a treasure trove of information for you, if you only ask. *Publishers Weekly* is a great source of information on sales figures—but it doesn't usually report on books returned, just books shipped. And if you didn't already know, the best-seller lists are based on books shipped, not sold.

A bookseller can tell you what's hot and what's not, at least in her store. What categories are hungriest for new material. What's bombing, despite the hype. What's drawing interest (and preorders) from the customers even before it gets to the shelf. What type of customer reads which type of book (you may be very surprised in some cases).

And that's just scratching the surface. We may be writers, but we are made or broken at the bookstore. Doesn't it follow that having a friend with her finger on the pulse of the book selling business is a worthwhile pursuit?

So go make a friend.

15.1.4 Writer's Parties

Parties?

"Writer" is often right up there with lighthouse keeper and Forest Service firewatcher in the isolation and loneliness department. By virtue of the very nature of writing, a writer works alone and apart.

When a writer throws a party, it's likely that there'll be other writers at the shindig. And what do writers talk about?

You've got it: They talk shop, just like professionals in any field. As you get to know more writers in your area, you will in all probability be invited to their parties. Go, and make contacts to your heart's content.

And if you can't find somebody throwing a party for writers, throw one yourself.

15.1.5   Arts Events

The least you'll find here is a collection of kindred spirits roaming through the teeming crowd. But artists attract people interested in the arts, and people interested in other arts. You never know, do you? At an awards reception honoring director Gus Van Sant a few years ago, we ran into at least a half-dozen writers we knew from the area, who'd attended to honor Van Sant, eat some free food, and schmooze.

15.1.6   Grocery Stores

Bet you didn't think of this one, did you?

You may run into the opportunity to hone your networking skills wherever you may be. We've met other writers in such diverse places as bars (big surprise there, huh?), laundromats, and river banks.

The rules remain the same, no matter where the contact is made.

Ask questions. People like to talk about something that excites them, especially if it's something they are doing personally, such as writing. Questions—intelligent, probing (but not prying) questions— open the door for them to talk about themselves.

Shut up and listen. You will always learn more with your mouth closed and your ears open than you will the other way around. Nature abhors a vacuum, and human nature abhors the vacuum of silence. When you shut up, the other person is most likely going to fill in the void, and this is your opportunity to learn.

Exchange business cards. Yes, even on a river bank. We always have a full business card holder with us, since our cards won't do us a bit of good if they just ride around in our pockets, getting mutilated, or sit on a shelf at home. Business cards are little pieces of memory that fit easily in our pockets, and it's always better to have them with you and not need them, than to not have them and need them. And we've passed them out in some of the *strangest* places.

Make notes (on the back of the other person's business card, after the conversation is over, just as we advised you to do at the conference). No matter where the contact occurs, it's still very important to remember all the salient details of the conversation if it does, indeed, come up again later.

Begin the process of making friends. Sometimes—often, in fact—this is as far as it goes. The person becomes an acquaintance, but not a friend. We're not being cold-hearted here. It's just that some people are true friendship material for us and others are not. We won't force a friendship where there's insufficient fuel. Either way, the process begins the same way. The door to friendship is opened, and the person has the opportunity to walk through. Some do. Some don't.

Whether the person becomes a friend, or just a friendly acquaintance, is immaterial—at least on a professional level. The important thing is that the contact is made and the person becomes an available source of information.

15.2 *You Hold the Key; Use It*

As we've shown you throughout this book, the process of networking is a two-way street. You've got to be willing to give if you're going to get. If your new friend (or acquaintance) asks you for information, and that information is yours to give, and that information will not cut your own throat if it gets out, give it!

Start the process of networking yourself. *Never leave it up to the other person to make the first move.* It's your business. It's your career. It's your destiny. So it's up to you to take control of your own situation. Nobody else can do it for you. Offer your help to someone else if you can, as well as asking for information from others if you need it.

In short, establish yourself as a person who realizes the tremendous importance of networking and holds the key to making it work. Lead, don't follow, the relationship to a mutually satisfying situation.

What we hope we've done here is expose you to a basis of information, a foundation you can build on in your own style. Starting today, you know enough to start building your own working network of friends and acquaintances who will help you build your business. Good luck.

Writer's Conferences and Workshops

WE'VE COMPILED THIS LIST of conferences and workshops that were available in 1994/1995 from a number of sources listed in the Bibliography, primarily to give you an idea of how much is available to you. By the time you read this, some of this information will be outdated—it's a fact of life that the publishing industry is fast changing. Use this list as a starting point to figure out which conferences you should attend. As always, the rest is up to you.

If your state isn't represented, don't despair. Contact local writing organizations, check the arts listings in your local newspaper, ask employees at your favorite bookstore, and call other writers you know in the area. In addition, if you live within commuting distance of another state, check for conferences across the border. At least one of these options should pay off.

ALABAMA

Alabama Writers' Conclave, 3225 Burning Tree Drive, Birmingham, Alabama 35226. August.

Con*Stellation, Orion, Box 4857, Huntsville, Alabama 35815. November.

DeepSouthCon, Box 94151, Birmingham, Alabama 35220. August.

Sea Oats Writer's Conference, Box 16101, Mobile, Alabama 36616; 205/343-8235. April.

Society of Children's Book Writers & Illustrators (SCBWI) Fall Conference, 1616 Kestwick Drive, Birmingham, Alabama 35226. October.

Southern Christian Writers' Conference (in Birmingham), Box 1106, Northport, Alabama 35476. June.

Writing Today/Birmingham-Southern College, Box A-3, Birmingham, Alabama 35254; 205/226-4921. April.

ALASKA

Alaska Adventure in Travel Writing, Box 21494, Juneau, Alaska 99802; 907/586-3067. June.

Midnight Sun Writers' Conference, University of Alaska/Fairbanks, English Department, Fairbanks, Alaska 99775; 907/474-7193. September.

Sitka Symposium, Box 2420, Sitka, Alaska 99835; 907/747-3794. June.

ARIZONA

American Christian Writers (multiple locations), Box 5168, Phoenix, Arizona 85010; 602/838-4919. Various.

Arizona Authors' Association, 3509 E. Shea Boulevard, Suite 117, Phoenix, Arizona 85018-1236; 602/942-4240. Various.

Arizona Christian Writers Conference, Box 5168, Phoenix, Arizona 85010; 602/838-4919. November.

Leprecon, Box 26665, Tempe, Arizona 85285; 602/945-6809. May.

Living History Time Seminars, Box 5318, Bisbee, Arizona 85603. May–December.

Phoenix Desert Rose Annual Conference (in Tempe), 6117 E. Hobart Drive, Mesa, Arizona 85205; 602/396-4018. September.

Pima Writers' Workshop, 2202 W. Anklam Road, Tucson, Arizona 85709; 602/884-6974. May.

Society of Southwestern Authors Writers' Conference, Box 30355, Tucson, Arizona 85751-0355; 602/795-0571. January.

Tus-Con, Box 26822, Tucson, Arizona 85726. November.

ARKANSAS

Arkansas Writers' Conference, Pioneer Branch/National League of American Pen Women, 1115 Gillette Drive, Little Rock, Arkansas 72207; 501/225-0166. June.

Ozark Creative Writers, 6817 Gingerbread Lane, Little Rock, Arkansas 72204; 501/565-8889. October.

Roc-Kon, Box 24285, Little Rock, Arkansas 72221. April–May.

CALIFORNIA

Bay Area Writers Workshop, Box 620327, Woodside, California 94062; 415/851-4568. Various.

Baycon, Box 10367, San Jose, California 95157. May.

Be the Writer You Want to Be Manuscript Clinic, 23350 Sereno Court, Villa 30, Cupertino, California 95014; 415/691-0300. Various.

Book Passage's Mystery Writers' Conference, 51 Tamal Vista Boulevard, Corte Madera, California 94925; 415/927-0960. July.

Book Passage's Travel Writers' Conference, 51 Tamal Vista Boulevard, Corte Madera, California 94925; 415/927-0960. August.

Book Publishing Workshop, Box 4232-61, Santa Barbara, California 93140-4232; 805/968-7277. April, September, November.

California Writers' Club Conference (in Pacific Grove), 2214 Derby Street, Berkeley, California 94705; 510/841-1217. June.

The Changing Landscapes of Indexing, 500 Hotel Circle N., San Diego, California 92108; 512/749-4052. May.

Christian Communicators' Conference (in Santa Clarita), 3133 Puente Street, Fullerton, California 92635; 800/959-6737. July.

Con-Chord, 13261 Donegal Drive, Garden Grove, California 92644. October.

Con-Dor, Box 15771, San Diego, California 92175; 619/447-6311. February.

Consonance, Wail Songs, Box 29888, Oakland, California 94604. March.

Contact, Box 506, Capitola, California 95010-0506. March.

Creative Communications Writing Conferences (in San Diego), Creative Communications, Box 2201, La Jolla, California 92038; 619/459-8897. January.

Foothills Writers' Conference, English Department, Foothills College, Los Altos Hills, California 94022; 415/949-7450. June.

Gene Perret's Round Table Comedy Writers Convention (in Palm Springs), 2135 Huntington Drive, #205, San Marino, California 91108; 818/796-4823. July.

Getting Your Book in the News Workshop, Gaughen Public Relations, 226 B-103 E. Canon Perdido Street, Santa Barbara, California 93101; 805/965-8482. Various.

How to Get and Stay Published, Box 26568, Fresno, California 93729-6568; 209/224-3564. April.

How to Self-Publish Your Own Book: Preparation and Production (various locations), Communications Unlimited, Box 6405, Santa Maria, California 93456; 805/937-8711. Various.

How to Sell 75% of Your Freelance Writing (various locations), Communications Unlimited, Box 6405, Santa Maria, California 93456; 805/937-8711. Various.

Idyllwild School of Music & the Arts, Box 38, Idyllwild, California 92549; 909/659-2171, x.4. June–August.

Investigative Reporters and Editors Computer-Assisted Reporting Conference (in San Jose, California), 100 Neff Hall, University of Missouri School of Journalism, Columbia, Missouri 65201; 314/882-2042. October.

I've Always Wanted to Write But . . . , 23350 Sereno Court, Villa 30, Cupertino, California 95014; 415/691-0300. Various.

Jack London Writers' Conference, 1500 Ralston Avenue, Belmont, California 94403; 415/508-3708. March.

Loscon, LASFS, 11513 Burbank Boulevard N., Hollywood, California 91601; 818/366-3827. November.

Making Orbit, 4009 Everett Avenue, Oakland, California 94602. January.

Mastering the Media Workshops, Desmond Communications, Box 30153, Santa Barbara, California 93130; 805/687-5596 or 800/448-3338. Various.

Mendocino Coast Writers Conference, 1211 Del Mar Drive, Ft. Bragg, California 95437; 707/961-1001. June.

Michael Hauge's Screenwriting for Hollywood (multiple locations), Hilltop Productions, Box 55728, Sherman Oaks, California 91413; 800/477-1947. Various.

Mt. Hermon Christian Writers Conference, Box 413, Mt. Hermon, California 95041; 408/335-4466. March.

Napa Valley Writers' Conference, Napa Valley College, 2277 Napa-Vallejo Highway, Napa, California 94558; 707/253-3070. August.

On Miracle Ground: The International Lawrence Durrell Conference (University of San Diego), Department of English and Philosophy, Georgia Southern University, Landrum Box 8032, Stateboro, Georgia 30460-8032. June.

Pasadena Writers' Forum, PCC Community Education Department, 1570 E. Colorado Boulevard, Pasadena, California 91106-2003; 818/585-7602. March.

Paul Gilette's Writing Workshop, 3284 Barham Boulevard, Suite 201, Los Angeles, California 90068-1454; 213/876-7590. Various.

Quantum Con, Box 93819, Pasadena, California 91109. February.

Robert McKee's Story Structure, Pacific Design Center, 12021 Wilshire Boulevard, Suite 868, Los Angeles, California 90025; 310/312-1002. Various.

San Diego County Writers' Guild Christian Writing Seminar, Box 1171, El Cajon, California 92022; 619/748-0565. September.

San Diego One-Day Christian Writers' Seminar, 14140 Mazatlan Court, Poway, California 92064; 619/748-0565. September.

San Diego State University Writers' Conference, SDSU-Aztec Center, San Diego, California 92182-0723; 619/594-2517. January.

Santa Barbara Publishing Workshop, Box 40500, Santa Barbara, California 93140-0500; 805/968-7277. May, August, November.

Santa Barbara Writers' Conference, Box 304, Carpinteria, California 93014; 805/684-2250. June.

SCBWI/Los Angeles Writers Conference in Children's Literature, Box 66296, Mar Vista Station, Los Angeles, California 90066; 818/347-2849. August.

SCBWI/Norcal Retreat at Asilomar (in Monterey), 1316 Rebecca Drive, Suisun, California 94585-3603; 707/426-6776. February.

SCBWI/Southern California Writers' Day, 11943 Montana, Los Angeles, California 90049; 310/820-5601. April.

Screenwriting Seminar, University of California/Davis Extension, 1333 Research Park Drive, Davis, California 95616-8727; 916/757-8895. Unspecified.

Self-Publishing Success Seminar (in Anaheim), Publisher Media, Box 1295, El Cajon, California 92022; 619/588-2155. May.

Selling to Hollywood (in Glendale), Writers Connection, Box 24770, San Jose, California 95154; 408/445-3600. August.

Society of Children's Book Writers and Illustrators (SCBWI) (sites vary), 22736 Vanowen Street, Suite 106, West Hills, California 91307; 818/888-8760. August.

Southern California Writers' Conference, 2596 Escondido Avenue, San Diego, California 92123; 619/278-4099. January.

Squaw Valley Community of Writers Workshops, Box 2352, Olympic Valley, California 96146; 916/583-5200. July, August.

Travel Writing—Make Your Vacation Pay for Itself (various locations), Villa 30, 23350 Sereno, Cupertino, California 95014; 408/741-2096. Various.

Two Day Film School for Writers (multiple locations), Box 481252, Los Angeles, California 90048; 800/355-3456. Various.

UC/Davis Writing Workshops, University Extension, Davis, California 95616; 916/757-8895. Various.

UC/Irvine Extension Writers' Conference, Department of Arts & Humanities, UCI Extension, Box 6050, Irvine, California 92716; 714/856-5414. July.

UCLA Extension Writers' Program, 10995 Le Conte Avenue, Los Angeles, California 90024; 310/825-9415 or 800/388-UCLA. Various.

West Marin Writers' Conference (in Point Reyes), Suite 201, #1 Weatherly Drive, Mill Valley, California 94941; 415/381-6671. July.

Write Your Life Story for Pay, 23350 Sereno Court, Villa 30, Cupertino, California 95014; 415/691-0300. Various.

Writing Children's Picture Books (in Sunnyvale), Writers Connection, Box 24770, San Jose, California 95154; 408/445-3600. May.

Writing for Children and Young Adults, 1122-26 E. Garfield Avenue, Glendale, California 91205; 818/548-0864. Spring.

Writing for Interactive Multimedia, Writers Connection, Box 24770, San Jose, California 95154; 408/445-3600. June.

Writing Travel Articles, Box 24770, San Jose, California 95154-4770; 408/445-3600. April.

Writing Travel Articles That Sell (various locations), Communications Unlimited, Box 6405, Santa Maria, California 93456; 805/937-8711. Various.

COLORADO

Aspen Writers' Conference, Drawer 7726, Aspen, Colorado 81615; 303/925-3122. June.

Colorado Christian Writers' Conference, 2801 Jay Road, Boulder, Colorado 80301; 303/823-5718. March.

Conference on the Literatures of the Fantastic, Sigma Tau Delta, English Department, University of Northern Colorado, Greeley, Colorado 80639. October.

Flatiron Genre Fiction Intensive with Bruce Holland Rogers, Continuing Education, Campus Box 178, University of Colorado, Boulder, Colorado 80309-0178; 303/492-5148. June.

Healing Through Writing & Selling Your Work, 4559 Beachcomber Court, Boulder, Colorado 80301; 303/530-1090. September.

The Jack Kerouac School of Disembodied Poetics Summer Writing Program, 2130 Arapahoe, Boulder, Colorado 80302; 303/444-0202. July.

MileHiCon, Box 27074, Lakewood, Colorado 80227; 303/426-0806. October.

National Writers Association, Suite 424, 1450 S. Havana, Aurora, Colorado 80012; 303/751-7844. June.

Nature Within, 26767 County Road 12, Somerset, Colorado 81434; 303/929-6575. July.

Peter Davidson's Writers' Seminar, Adult Education, Morgan Community College, 17800 Road 20, Ft. Morgan, Colorado 80701; 800/622-0216 x.110 or 303/867-3081 x.110. August.

Peter Davidson's Writers' Seminar, Box 33, Division of Extended Studies, Pikes Peak Community College, 5675 S. Academy Boulevard, Colorado Springs, Colorado 80906; 800/825-0401 x.7230 or 719/576-7711 x.7230. July.

Peter Davidson's Writers' Seminar, Continuing Education, Arapahoe Community College, 2500 W. College Drive, Littleton, Colorado 80120; 303/797-5722. July.

Pikes Peak Writers' Conference, Box 25417, Colorado Springs, Colorado 80936-5417. April.

Rocky Mountain Fiction Writers/Colorado Gold, Box 260244, Denver, Colorado 80226-0244; 303/791-3941. September.

SCBWI/Rocky Mountain Fall/Winter Workshops, 8600 Firethorn Drive, Loveland, Colorado 80538; 303/669-3755. September, February, May.

SCBWI/Rocky Mountain Summer Retreat, 1712 Morning Drive, Loveland, Colorado 80538; 303/667-2793. July.

The Springs Writers' Conference for Adults, Colorado Christian Communicators, 5209 Del Paz Drive, Colorado Springs, Colorado 80918. June.

The Springs Writers' Conference for Children, Colorado Christian Communicators, 5209 Del Paz Drive, Colorado Springs, Colorado 80918. June.

The Springs Writers' Conference for Teens, Colorado Christian Communicators, 5209 Del Paz Drive, Colorado Springs, Colorado 80918. June.

Steamboat Springs Writers Group, Box 774284, Steamboat Springs, Colorado 80477; 303/879-9008. Summer.

Sustained Inspiration for Writers with Bruce Holland Rogers, Continuing Education, Campus Box 178, University of Colorado, Boulder, Colorado 80309-0178; 303/492-5148. June.

Vail Writers' Retreat (in Vail, Colorado), 1200 Midland Building, Des Moines, Iowa 50309; 800/551-9453. July.

Write Today, Sell Tomorrow (in Denver), 1450 S. Havana, Suite 424, Aurora, Colorado 80012; 303/751-7844. June.

Writers in the Rockies TV and Film Screenwriting Conference, 1980 Glenwood Drive, Boulder, Colorado 80304; 303/443-4636. August.

CONNECTICUT

Deaf Playwrights Conference, National Theatre of the Deaf, 5 W. Main Street, Chester, Connecticut 06412; 203/526-4971 or 203/526-4974 (TDD). June.

Wesleyan Writers Conference, Wesleyan University, Middletown, Connecticut 06459; 203/343-3938. June.

DISTRICT OF COLUMBIA

Education Writers Association (sites vary), 1001 Connecticut Avenue NW, Suite 310, Washington, DC 20036; 202/429-9680. April.

Gaylaxicon, Box 656, Washington, DC 20044. July.

How to Write and Sell a Movie (in Washington, DC), 3113 N. Pershing Drive, Arlington, Virginia 22201; 703/528-6273. May, October, November.

National League of American Pen Women (sites vary), Pen Arts Building, 1300 17 Street NW, Washington, DC 20036; 202/785-1997. April.

Society of American Travel Writers (sites vary), 1155 Connecticut Avenue NW, Suite 500, Washington, DC 20036; 202/429-6639. October.

Washington Independent Writers Spring Writers Conference, #220, 733 15th Street NW, Washington, DC 20005; 202/347-4973. May.

FLORIDA

Christian Writers Conference (sites vary), 177 E. Crystal Lake Avenue, Lake Mary, Florida 32746; 407/324-5465. June.

Florida Christian Writers Conference, 2600 Park Avenue, Titusville, Florida 32780; 407/269-6702. January.

Florida First Coast Writers' Festival, Florida Community College/Jacksonville, 4501 Capper Road, Jacksonville, Florida 32218; 904/766-6559. April.

Florida Freelance Writers Association (in Orlando, Florida), Maple Ridge Road, North Sandwich, New Hampshire 03259; 603/254-6367. May.

Florida State Writers Conference (in Florida), CNW, Maple Ridge Road, North Sandwich, New Hampshire 03259; 603/284-6367. May.

Florida Suncoast Writers' Conference, University of South Florida/St. Petersburg Campus, 140 7th Avenue South, St. Petersburg, Florida 33701; 813/974-1711. January–February.

Hemingway Days Writer's Workshop and Conference, Box 4045, Key West, Florida 33041; 305/294-4440. July.

International Conference on the Fantastic, College of Humanities, 500 NW 20th, HU-50 B-9, Florida Atlantic University, Boca Raton, Florida 33431; 717/532-1495. March.

Key West Literary Seminar, 419 Petronia Street, Key West, Florida 33040; 305/293-9291. January.

Mystery Writers of America's Sleuth Fest (in Ft. Lauderdale), Levitt Entertainment, 9400 SW 63 Court, Miami, Florida 33156; 305/663-8997. March.

Necronomicon, Box 2076, Riverview, Florida 33569; 813/677-6347. October.

Oasis, Box 940922, Maitland, Florida 32794; 904/788-6727. May.

Sarasota Festival of New Plays, Florida Studio Theatre, 1241 N. Palm Avenue, Sarasota, Florida 34236; 813/366-9017. May.

Southwest Florida Writers' Conference, Box 60210, Ft. Myers, Florida 33919; 813/489-9226. February.

Space Coast Writers Guild Conference, Box 804, Melbourne, Florida 32902; 407/727-0051. November.

Tropicon, Box 70143, Ft. Lauderdale, Florida 33307; 305/385-4111. January.

Write for Success Workshop: Children's Books, 3748 Harbor Heights Drive, Largo, Florida 34644; 813/581-2484. Irregularly.

Write for Success Workshop: Fiction & Film (in Clearwater, Florida); 813/481-3484. May.

Writers Workshop in Children's Literature, SCBWI/Florida, 2000 Springdale Boulevard, Apt. F-103, Palm Springs, Florida 33461; 407/433-1727. September.

GEORGIA

Council of Authors & Journalists, Inc. (in Athens), Box 830008, Stone Mountain, Georgia 30083-0001. July.

Curry Hill Plantation Writer's Retreat (near Bainbridge, Georgia), 404 Crestmont Avenue, Hattiesburg, Mississippi 39401-7211; 601/264-7034. March.

Dragon*Con, Box 47696, Atlanta, Georgia 30362. July.

Emory Summer Writing Institute, English Department, Emory University, Atlanta, Georgia 30322; 404/727-5798. July–August.

Moonlight and Magnolias Writer's Conference, 4128 Manson Avenue, Smyrna, Georgia 30082; 404/432-4860. October.

Mothers, Daughters, Grandmothers—Writing the Autobiography in Your Own Words, The International Women's Writing Guild, Box 810, Gracie Station, New York, New York 10028. October.

Progoff Intensive Journal Workshop, Box 337, Rabun Gap, Georgia 30568; 706/746-5718. May.

Sandhills Writers' Conference, Augusta College, Continuing Education, 2500 Walton Way, Augusta, Georgia 30910; 706/737-1636. May.

Savannah Writers' Retreat (in Savannah, Georgia), 1200 Midland Building, Des Moines, Iowa 50309; 800/551-9453. May.

Southeastern Writers Association Annual Workshop, 4021 Gladesworth Lane, Decatur, Georgia 30035; 404/288-2064. June.

Southeastern Writers Conference, Route 1, Box 102, Cuthbert, Georgia 31740; 912/679-5445. June.

HAWAII

Hands-On Writer's Workshop (in Kona, Hawaii), Box 1380, Lindale, Texas 75771; 903/882-9172, x.288. July.

Maui Writers' Conference, #38, 20 Alaeloa, Lahaina, Maui 96761; 800/262-8440. September.

ILLINOIS

Autumn Authors' Affair (in Lisle), 1507 Burnham Avenue, Calumet City, Illinois 60409; 708/862-9797. October.

Blooming Grove Writers' Conference, Box 515, Bloomington, Illinois 61702; 309/828-5092. August.

Breaking into Magazine Writing (various Illinois sites); 815/654-4295 or 708/858-2800. Various.

Of Dark & Stormy Nights, Mystery Writers of America/Midwest, 200 S. Garden Avenue, Roselle, Illinois 60172; 708/980-9535. June.

International Black Writers Conference, Box 1030, Chicago, Illinois 60690; 312/924-3818. June.

Mississippi Valley Writers Conference, Augustana College, Rock Island, Illinois 61201; 309/762-8985. June.

Northern Illinois Writers Conference, 215 N. Wyman Street, Rockford, Illinois 61101; 815/965-6731. June.

Progress in the Pressroom Seminar (in Chicago), Research & Engineering Council of the Graphic Arts Industry, Inc., Box 639, Chadds Ford, Pennsylvania 19317; 215/388-7394. December.

The Society of Midland Authors, 29 E. Division Street, Chicago, Illinois 60610; 312/337-1482. May.

WindyCon, Box 184, Palatine, Illinois 60078-0184. November.

The World of Freelance Writing (various Illinois sites); 708/858-2800. Various.

Write to Publish Conference (in Chicago), #6F, 9731 Fox Glen Drive, Niles, Illinois 60714; 800/959-6737. June.

Writing from an Interview (various Illinois sites); 708/858-2800 or 815/654-4295. Various.

INDIANA

Association of Great Lakes Outdoor Writers (sites vary), 301 N. Cross Street, Sullivan, Indiana 47882-1419; 812/268-6232. September.

Charlene Faris Seminars for Beginners, 9524 Guilford Drive, #A, Indianapolis, Indiana 46240; 317/848-2634. Spring, Fall.

InConJunction, Box 19776, Indianapolis, Indiana 46219. July.

Midwest Writers Workshop, Department of Journalism, Ball State University, Muncie, Indiana 47306; 317/285-8200. July.

The Society of Professional Journalists (sites vary), Box 77, Greencastle, Indiana 46135; 317/653-3333. October.

Write to the Point (in Warsaw), 5242 S 1000 W., Mentone, Indiana 46539; 219/353-8140. October.

IOWA

Icon, Box 525, Iowa City, Iowa 52244; 319/351-8200. October.

Iowa Summer Writing Festival, 116 International Center, University of Iowa, Iowa City, Iowa 52242; 319/335-2534. June–July.

Midwest Writers' Retreat, 900 Midland Building, Lake Okoboji, Iowa 50309; 800/551-9453. June.

Peter Davidson's Children's Picture Book Seminar, Adult & Continuing Education, NE Iowa Community College, 10250 Sundown Road, Peosta, Iowa 52068; 319/556-5110. July.

Peter Davidson's Writers' Seminar, Adult Education, Scott Community College, 500 Belmont Road, Bettendorf, Iowa 52722; 319/359-4141. July.

Sinipee Writers' Workshop, Box 902, Dubuque, Iowa 52004-0902; 319/556-0366. April.

KANSAS

Heart of America Writers' Conference, 12345 College Boulevard, Overland Park, Kansas 66210. April.

Novelists, Inc. Annual National Conference, Box 1166, Mission, Kansas 66222. October.

Peter Davidson's Children's Picture Book Seminar, Adult Education, Dodge City Community College, US 50 Bypass at 14 Avenue, Dodge City, Kansas 67801; 316/227-9295. July.

Peter Davidson's Writers' Seminar, Barton County Community College, RR 3, Great Bend, Kansas 67530; 316/792-2701, x.214. July.

Peter Davidson's Writers' Seminar, Community Education, Cloud County Community College, 2221 Campus Drive, Concordia, Kansas 66901; 913/243-1435. July.

Writers Workshop in Science Fiction, English Department/University of Kansas, Lawrence, Kansas 66045; 913/864-3380. July.

KENTUCKY

Appalachian Writers' Workshop, Box 844, Hindman, Kentucky 41822; 606/785-5475. July–August.

Creative Writing Conference, English Department, Eastern Kentucky University, Richmond, Kentucky 40475; 606/622-5861. June.

Green River Novels-in-Progress Workshop, 11906 Locust Road, Louisville, Kentucky 40243; 502/245-4902. January.

Green River Writers Summer Retreat (in Louisville), 403 S. 6th Street, Ironton, Kentucky 45638; 614/533-1081. July.

The National Society of Newspaper Columnists, Box 22668, Louisville, Kentucky 40252; 816/234-4141 or 512/582-4646. Various.

Shawnee Hills Spring Poetry Workshop (in Greenup, Kentucky), 403 S. 6th Street, Ironton, Ohio 45638; 614/533-1081. April–May.

A Touch of Success Writing Workshop for Photographers (at Oakbrook Farm, Kentucky), Box 194, Lowell, Florida 32663; 904/867-0463 or 502/769-1823. September.

University of Kentucky Women Writers Conference, 202 Patterson Office Tower, University of Kentucky, Lexington, Kentucky 40506-0027; 606/357-6681. October.

Writers' Voice of the YMCA of Central Kentucky Writers' Workshops, 251 W. 2nd Street, Lexington, Kentucky 40507. September, October, November.

Writing Workshop for People over 57, Donovan Scholars Program, Ligon House, University of Kentucky, Lexington, Kentucky 40506-0442; 606/257-8314. June.

LOUISIANA

Belles, Beaux, and Bayous, 43 Westwood Boulevard, Alexandria, Louisiana 71301; 318/487-9917. May.

Deep South Writers Conference, Drawer 44691, Lafayette, Louisiana 70504-4691; 318/231-6918. September.

Deep South Writers Conference, University of SW Louisiana, USL Box 44691, Lafayette, Louisiana 70504; 318/231-6000 or 318/231-6908. September.

MAINE

Down East Maine Writer's Workshop (in Camden/Belfast), Box 446, Stockton Springs, Maine 04981; 207/567-4317. October.

The International Film Workshops, 2 Central Street, Rockport, Maine 04856; 207/236-8581. Summer.

State of Maine Writers' Conference, Box 296, Ocean Park, Maine 04063; 207/934-5034, June–August; 413/596-6734, September–May. August.

Stonecoast Writers' Conference, Summer Session Office, University of Southern Maine, 96 Falmouth Street, Portland, Maine 04103; 207/280-4076. July–August.

Wells Writers' Workshops (in Wells, Maine), 69 Broadway, Concord, New Hampshire 03301; 603/225-9162. May, September.

MARYLAND

American Medical Writers Association (sites vary), 9650 Rockville Pike, Bethesda, Maryland 20814; 301/493-0003. November.

Balticon, Box 686, Baltimore, Maryland 21203. April.

Darkover Grand Council Meeting, Box 7203, Silver Spring, Maryland 20907; 202/737-4609. November.

The Literary Festivals at St. Mary's College of Maryland: Poetry & Fiction, St. Mary's College of Maryland, St. Mary's City, Maryland; 301/862-0129. May–June.

National Conference of Editorial Writers (sites vary), 6223 Executive Boulevard, Rockville, Maryland 20852; 301/984-3015. September.

National Federation of Press Women (sites vary), Box 99, 1105 Main Street, Blue Springs, Maryland 64013; 816/229-1666. June.

SCBWI/Writers' Retreat (in Cumberland, Maryland), Box 66296, Mar Vista Station, Los Angeles, California 90066. July.

MASSACHUSETTS

Arisia, 1 Kendall Square, #322, Cambridge, Massachusetts 02139; 617/364-1576. January.

Become a More Productive Writer, Creative Ways, Box 1310, Boston, Massachusetts 02117; 617/266-1613. May.

Book Manufacturing Seminar, Book Manufacturers' Institute, 45 William Street, Wellesley, Massachusetts 02181; 617/239-0103. October.

Boskone, NESFA, Box 809, Framingham, Massachusetts 01701. February.

Cape Literary Arts Workshop, Cape Cod Conservatory, Route 132, West Barnstable, Massachusetts 02668; 508/775-4811. Various.

Eastern Writers' Conference, English Department, Salem State College, Salem, Massachusetts 01970; 508/741-6330. June.

Gary Provost's Writers' Retreat Workshop (multiple locations), Box 139, South Lancaster, Massachusetts 01561; 800/642-2494. Various.

Harvard Summer Writing Program, 51 Brattle Street, Cambridge, Massachusetts 02138. June–August.

Lexington Motion Pictures Seminar, 218 Bedford Street, Lexington, Massachusetts 02173. October.

Martha's Vineyard Writers' Workshop, The Nathan Mayhew Seminars of Martha's Vineyard, Inc., Box 1125, Vineyard Haven, Massachusetts 02568; 508/693-6603. Summer.

Mt. Holyoke Writers' Conference, Box 3213-W, Mt. Holyoke College, South Hadley, Massachusetts 01075; 413/538-2308. June.

New England Writers' Workshop at Simmons College, 300 The Fenway, Boston, Massachusetts 02115; 617/521-2088. June.

Perspectives in Children's Literature, 226 Furcolo Hall, University of Massachusetts, Amherst, Massachusetts 01003-3035; 413/545-4325. April.

Procrastination: Creative Solutions for Writers, Creative Ways, Box 1310, Boston, Massachusetts 02117; 617/266-1613. June.

A Publicity Primer for Writers, Creative Ways, Box 1310, Boston, Massachusetts 02117; 617/266-1613. April.

University of Massachusetts/Lowell Writing Program, One University Avenue, Lowell, Massachusetts 01854; 508/934-2405. July–August.

Writing with Your Whole Self, Box 1310, Boston, Massachusetts 02117; 617/266-1613. Various.

MICHIGAN

Clarion Science Fiction & Fantasy Writing Workshop, Lyman Briggs School, E-28 Holmes Hall, Michigan State University, East Lansing, Michigan 48825-1107; 517/353-7196. Summer.

ConClave, Box 2915, Ann Arbor, Michigan 48106. October.

ConFusion, Box 8284, Ann Arbor, Michigan 48107. January.

Engineering Conferences: Writing Instructions, Procedures and Documentation, University of Michigan, Chrysler Center, North Campus, Ann Arbor, Michigan 48109; 313/764-8490. Summer.

Maranatha Christian Writers' Seminar, Maranatha Bible & Missionary Conference Grounds, 4759 Lake Harbor Road, Muskegon, Michigan 49441; 616/798-2161. August.

Midland Writers Conference, Grace A. Dow Memorial Library, 1710 W. St. Andrews, Midland, Michigan 48640; 517/835-7151. June.

National Small Press Book Publishing Institute (in Traverse City), 6893 Sullivan Road, Grawn, Michigan 49637; 616/276-5196, x.103. April.

Oakland University Writers' Conference, 265 SFH, Rochester, Michigan 48309-4401; 313/370-3120. October.

Third Coast Writers' Conference, Department of English, Western Michigan University, Kalamazoo, Michigan 49008-5092; 616/387-2570. May.

Thunder Bay Literary Conference, 211 N. 1st Street, Alpena, Michigan; 517/356-6188. September.

MINNESOTA

Arcana, 3136 Park Avenue S., Minneapolis, Minnesota 55405-1525. September.

Diversicon, Box 8036, Minneapolis, Minnesota 55408. August.

Lakewood Community College Writers' Seminar, 3401 Century Avenue, White Bear Lake, Minnesota 55110; 612/779-3259. Fall, Winter, Spring.

MiniCon (in Bloomington), Registration Department, Box 8297, Minneapolis, Minnesota 55408; 612/333-7533. April.

Peter Davidson's Children's Picture Book Seminar, Continuing Education, Anoka-Ramsey Community College, 11200 Mississippi Boulevard NW, Coon Rapids, Minnesota 55433; 612/422-3419. June.

Peter Davidson's Writers' Seminar, Continuing Education, Lakewood Community College, 3401 Century Avenue N., White Lake, Minnesota 55110; 612/779-3341. June.

SCBWI/Minnesota Workshop, 4042 24th Avenue S., Minneapolis, Minnesota 55406; 612/724-2097. Spring.

Split Rock Arts Program, University of Minnesota, 306 Westbrook Hall, 77 Pleasant Street SE, Minneapolis, Minnesota 55455; 612/624-6800. July, August.

Valleycon (in Moorhead, Minnesota), Box 7202, Fargo, North Dakota 58109; 701/280-1445 or 218/233-9550. October.

Writer's Seminar/Anoka-Ramsey Community College, 11200 Mississippi Boulevard NW, Coon Rapids, Minnesota 55345; 612/422-3301. Fall.

Writing to Sell, The Writers' Workshop, Box 24356, Minneapolis, Minnesota 55424. Various.

MISSISSIPPI

The Eudora Welty Film & Fiction Festival, Box 1278, Jackson, Mississippi 39215. May.

MISSOURI

Archon, Box 50125, Clayton, Missouri 63105. June.

Blended Voices: A Celebration of Creative Arts (in Kansas City), Box 8278, Prairie Village, Missouri 66208; 913/642-1503. June.

Contraception, Box 1046, Lee's Summit, Missouri 64063. October.

Fiction from the Heartland Conference, Box 32186, Kansas City, Missouri 64111. February.

Heartland Writers' Guild Conference (in Cape Girardeau), Box 652, Kennett, Missouri 63857; 314/888-3032 or 314/888-2995. Various.

Investigative Reporters and Editors National Conference (in St. Louis), 100 Neff Hall, University of Missouri School of Journalism, Columbia, Missouri 65211; 314/882-2042. June.

Maple Woods Community College Writer's Conference, 2601 NE Barry Road, Kansas City, Missouri 64156; 816/734-4878. October.

Mark Twain Writers Conference, Suite A, 921 Center, Hannibal, Missouri 63401; 800/747-0738. June.

Name That Con, Box 575, St. Charles, Missouri 63302. April.

SCBWI/Drury College Writing for Children Workshop, 900 N. Benton, Springfield, Missouri 65802; 417/865-8731. October.

SCBWI/Midwest Writer's Conference, 532 W. Jewel, Kirkwood, Missouri 63122; 314/965-4274. June.

Society of American Business Editors & Writers (sites vary), University of Missouri, Box 838, Columbia, Missouri 65205; 314/882-7862. May.

Writing for Radio with Tom Lopez of the ZBS Foundation, 915 E. Broadway, Columbia, Missouri 65201; 314/874-5676. June.

MONTANA

Environmental Writing Institute (at Teller Wildlife Refuge, Corvallis), Center for Continuing Education, University of Montana, Missoula, Montana 59812; 406/243-2094. May.

Fall/Spring Writers' Conference, 4949 2nd Avenue N., Great Falls, Montana 59406; 406/453-0256. October, April.

Miscon, Box 9363, Missoula, Montana 59807; 406/728-9423. April.

Yellow Bay Writers' Conference (at Flathead Lake), Center for Continuing Education, University of Montana, Missoula, Montana 59812; 406/243-2094. August.

NEBRASKA

Nebraska Writers Guild, Box 30341, Lincoln, Nebraska 68503-0341; 402/477-3804. April.

Peter Davidson's Children's Picture Book Seminar, Adult & Continuing Education, SE Community College, 8800 O Street, Lincoln, Nebraska 68520; 402/437-2705. July.

Peter Davidson's Writers' Seminar, Community Education, Central Community College, Box 4903, Grand Island, Nebraska 68802; 308/389-6442. July.

Peter Davidson's Writers' Seminar, Community Services, Mid-Plains Community College, McDonald-Beltoh Campus, Box 1, Route 4, North Platte, Nebraska 69101; 308/532-8980. August.

Reader's Digest Magazine Writing Workshop, 206 Avery Hall, University of Nebraska, Lincoln, Nebraska 68588-0127; 402-3041. May.

Romance Writers' and Readers' Conference, University of Nebraska/Omaha, Peter Kiewet Conference Center, 1313 Farnam Street, Omaha, Nebraska 68182; 402/595-2355. March.

NEVADA

Crimes, Crooks and Crime Scenes, 9333 Dry Dock Drive, Las Vegas, Nevada 89117; 702/254-1708. July.

SilverCon, Box 95941, Las Vegas, Nevada 89193. April.

NEW HAMPSHIRE

Festival of Poetry (at The Robert Frost Place), Ridge Road, Fraconia, New Hampshire 03580; 602/823-5510. August.

NEW JERSEY

Advanced Writing and Interviewing Workshop (multiple locations), 309 Windsor Terrace, Ridgewood, New Jersey 07450; 201/444-3147. Various.

New Jersey Writers' Conference, New Jersey Institute of Technology, Newark, New Jersey 07102; 201/596-3441 or 908/889-7336. March.

Trenton State College Writers' Conference, English Department, Trenton State College, Hillwood Lakes CN 4700, Trenton, New Jersey 08650-4700; 609/771-3254. Spring.

Writing by the Sea, 1511 New York Avenue, Cape May, New Jersey 08204; 609/884-7117 x.15. November.

The Writing Center, 601 Palisade Avenue, Englewood Cliffs, New Jersey 07632; 201/567-4017. Various.

NEW MEXICO

Gila Writers' Conference (in Silver City), 11012 E. Crescent Avenue, Apache Junction, New Mexico 85220; 602/986-1399. July.

Reader's Digest Writers Workshop (in Albuquerque), NAU Box 5638, Flagstaff, Arizona 86011; 602/523-3559. August.

Santa Fe Writers' Conference, 826 Camino de Monte Rey, Santa Fe, New Mexico 87501; 505/982-9301. August.

SW Christian Writers' Association, Box 2635, Farmington, New Mexico 87499-2635; 505/334-0617. September.

SW Writers Workshop, 1336 Wyoming Boulevard NE, Suite C, Albuquerque, New Mexico 87112-5000; 505/293-0303. September.

Taos Institute of Arts, Box 2469, Taos, New Mexico 87571; 505/758-2793. June–October.

NEW YORK

American Society of Journalists and Authors Writers' Conference, #302, 1501 Broadway, New York, New York 10036; 212/997-0947. June.

AstronomiCon, Box 1701, Rochester, New York 14603; 716/342-4697. March.

The Baker Street Irregulars (in New York City), 34 Pierson Avenue, Norwood, New Jersey 07648; 201/768-2241. January.

Book Producers Seminar, American Book Producers Association, 160 Fifth Avenue, New York, New York 10011-7000; 212/645-2368. October.

Breaking into TV and Film Scriptwriting, TV/Radio Department, 304 Whitehead, Brooklyn College, Brooklyn, New York 11210; 718/951-5555. June.

Brockport Writers' Forum, Department of English, SUNY-Brockport, Brockport, New York 14420. June–July.

Brooklyn Writers' Network Workshops, 2509 Avenue K, Brooklyn, New York 11210; 718/377-4945. Various.

Champlain Valley Nature Writers' Workshop (in Plattsburg), 40 W. Valley Road, Lake Placid, New York 12946; 518/523-1749. July.

Chautauqua Writers' Workshop, Box 1098, Chautauqua, New York 14722; 716/357-6255. July.

Children's Literature Writing Workshop, Writer's Voice Project, Silver Bay Association, Silver Bay, New York 12874; 518/543-8833. May.

Contradiction, Box 100, Bridge Station, Niagara Falls, New York 14305; 716/285-2290. November.

Copywriters Council of America/Freelance (sites vary), 7 Putter Lane, CCA Building 102, Middle Island, New York 11953-0102; 516/924-8555 x.203. November.

Cornell University Summer Session, B20 Day Hall, Ithaca, New York 14853-2801; 607/255-4987. Various.

Feminist Women's Writing Workshops, Box 6583, Ithaca, New York 14851. Summer.

Highlights Foundation Writers Workshop (in Chautauqua), 814 Court Street, Honesdale, New York 18431; 717/253-1192. July.

Hofstra University Summer Writers' Conference, 110 Hofstra University, UCCE, 205 Davison Hall, Hempstead, New York 11550; 516/463-5016. July.

How to Create Drama and Comedy That Works, #17G, 160 West End Avenue, New York, New York 10023; 212/362-5022. April–July.

I-Con, Box 550, Stony Brook, New York 11790. April.

Journal Writing Workshop, Writer's Voice Project, Silver Bay Association, Silver Bay, New York 12874; 518/543-8833. April.

LU1091—Summer Writers' Conference, 110 Hofstra University, Hempstead, New York 11550; 516/463-5016. July.

LunaCon, Box 3455, Church Street Station, New York, New York 10008. March.

Manhattanville College Writers' Week, 2900 Purchase Street, Purchase, New York 10577; 914/694-3425. June.

Marymount Manhattan College Writers' Conference, Continuing Education, Marymount Manhattan College, 221 E. 71st Street, New York, New York 10021; 212/517-0564. June.

Meet the Agents, International Women's Writing Guild, Box 810, Gracie Station, New York, New York 10028. October.

National Association of Science Writers (sites vary), Box 294, Greenlawn, New York 11740; 516/757-5664. February.

National Readings Tour, Writer's Voice Project, Silver Bay Association, Silver Bay, New York 12874; 518/543-8833. July, August.

Nature Writing Workshop, Writer's Voice Project, Silver Bay Association, Silver Bay, New York 12874; 518/543-8833. June.

New York State Writers Institute, State University of New York/Albany, 1400 Washington Avenue, Albany, New York 12222; 518/442-5620. Various.

The Poetry Society of America, 15 Gramercy Park, New York, New York 10003; 212/254-9628 or 212/254-9683. Various.

Poetry Writing Workshop, Writer's Voice Project, Silver Bay Association, Silver Bay, New York 12874; 518/543-8833. May.

Remember the Magic (in Saratoga Springs), International Women's Writing Guild, Box 810, Gracie Station, New York, New York 10028. August.

Robert McKee's Story Structure (in New York City), 12021 Wilshire Boulevard, Suite 868, Los Angeles, California 90025; 310/312-1002. June, September, December.

Robert Quackenbush's Children's Book Writing & Illustrating Workshops, 460 E. 79th Street, New York, New York 10021; 212/744-3822. July.

Romance Writers of America/New York City, Bowling Green Station, Box 1719, New York, New York 10274-1133; 718/441-5214. February.

Sarah Lawrence College Summer Seminars for Writers, 1 Mead Way, Bronxville, New York 10708-5999; 914/395-2373. June.

SCBWI/Hofstra Children's Literature Conference, Hofstra University, Continuing Education, 205 Davison Hall, Hempstead, New York 11550; 516/463-5016. April.

SCBWI/NYC Conference in Children's Literature, Box 20233, Park West Finance Station, New York, New York 10025-1511. November.

Science Fiction and Fantasy Writers of America (sites vary), 5 Winding Brook Drive, 1B, Guilderland, New York 12084. April.

Southampton Writers' Workshops & Festival, Long Island University/Southampton, Southampton, New York 11968; 516/287-8349. July.

SUNY College Writing Arts Festivals, SUNY/Oswego, Oswego, New York 13126; 315/341-2602. October, April.

Technical Writers' Institute, Office of Continuing Education, Rensselaer Polytechnic Institute, Troy, New York 12180-3590; 518/276-8351. June.

Vassar College Institute of Publishing and Writing: Children's Books in the Marketplace, Box 300, Poughkeepsie, New York 12601; 914/437-5903. June, July.

Westchester Writers' Conference, 16 Lawrence Drive, North White Plains, New York 10603; 914/682-1574. April.

Women's Writing Conferences & Retreats (multiple locations), International Women's Writing Guild, Box 810, Gracie Station, New York, New York 10028; 212/737-7536. Various.

Write Now Weekend Intensive Writing Workshop, #17G, 160 West End Avenue, New York, New York 10023; 212/362-5022. April–July.

Writers on Writing at Barnard, 3009 Broadway, New York, New York 10027-6598; 212/854-7489. June.

The Writers' Center at Chautauqua, Box 408, Chautauqua, New York 14722; 716/357-2445 or 717/872-8337. June–August.

Writers' Weekend, Lake Mohonk, New Paltz, New York 12561; 914/255-1000. April.

NORTH CAROLINA

Duke Creative Writers' Workshop (10th-11th graders), Duke Youth Programs, Box 90702, Durham, North Carolina 27709; 919/684-6259. August.

Duke University Writers' Workshop, The Bishop's House, Durham, North Carolina 27708; 919-684-3255. June.

Duke Young Writers' Camp (6th-11th graders), Duke Youth Programs, Box 90702, Durham, North Carolina 27709; 919/684-6259. June, July.

North Carolina Writers' Network Fall Conference, Box 954, Carrboro, North Carolina 27510; 919/967-9540. October, November.

"A Vision for Your Voice" (locations vary), North Carolina Writers Network, Box 954, Carrboro, North Carolina 27510; 919/967-9540. Various.

Wildacres Writers' Workshop (in Little Switzerland), 233 S. Elm Street, Greensboro, North Carolina 27401; 800/635-2049. July.

The Writers' Workshop (sites vary), Box 696, Asheville, North Carolina 28802; 800/627-0142. Various.

OHIO

Antioch Writers' Workshop of Yellow Springs, Box 494, Yellow Springs, Ohio 45387; 513/767-9112. July.

Cleveland Heights/University Heights Writers Mini Conference, #110, 34200 Ridge Road, Willoughby, Ohio 44094; 216/943-3047. November.

The Columbus Writers Conference, Box 20548, Columbus, Ohio 43220; 614/451-0216 or 614/326-2686. October.

Context, Box 2954, Columbus, Ohio 43216; 614/263-6089. October.

Imagination, Cleveland State University, Cleveland, Ohio 44115; 216/687-4522. July.

Marcon, Box 211101, Columbus, Ohio 43221; 614/451-3154. May.

Midwest Writers' Conference (at Kent State), 6000 Frank Avenue NW, Canton, Ohio 44720; 216/499-9600. October.

MilleniCon, Box 636, Dayton, Ohio 45405. March.

National Association of Agricultural Journalists (sites vary), 312 Valley View Drive, Huron, Ohio 44839; 419/433-5412. June.

OctoCon, 34 Creekwood Square, Glendale, Ohio 45246. October.

Ohio State's Summer Writing Series, 152 Mount Hall, 1050 Carmack Road, Columbus, Ohio 43210-1002; 614/292-2006. Summer.

Reading, Writing & Romance, 72 Cherokee Drive, Hamilton, Ohio 45013; 513/863-6053. February.

Skyline Writers' Conference, 8358 Ridge Road, North Royalton, Ohio 44133; 216/237-4493. August.

Tri C West Writers Conference, #110, 34200 Ridge Road, Willoughby, Ohio 44094; 216/943-3047. June.

Western Reserve Writers & Freelance Conference, #110, 34200 Ridge Road, Willoughby, Ohio 44094; 216/943-3047. September.

Writers Mini Conference, #110, 34200 Ridge Road, Willoughby, Ohio 44094; 216/943-3047. Various.

Writing & Marketing Feature Stories Workshop, Box 20548, Columbus, Ohio 43220; 614/451-0216 or 614/326-2686. May.

OKLAHOMA

Football Writers Association of America (sites vary), Box 1022, Edmond, Oklahoma 73083; 405/341-4731. June.

Oklahoma Fall Arts Institutes, Box 18154, Oklahoma City, Oklahoma 73154; 405/842-0890. October.

Professionalism in Writing School, A Conference for Christians Who Write, 4308 S. Peoria, Suite 701, Tulsa, Oklahoma 74105; 918/749-5588. March–April.

Short Course in Professional Writing, 860 Van Vleet Oval, Room 120, Norman, Oklahoma 73019-0270; 405/325-4171. June.

SoonerCon, Box 1701, Bethany, Oklahoma 73008; 405/682-6462. November.

OREGON

Coaching Writers' Conference (in Turner), 876 SE Christian Street, Myrtle Creek, Oregon 97457; 206/695-2263. August.

Columbia Gorge Writers' Conference, 2470 Lichens Drive, Hood River, Oregon 97031. April.

Finer Points Writers' Retreats (in Coos Bay), Box 534, Coquille, Oregon 97423. Various.

Haystack Writing Program (in Cannon Beach), Portland State University, Summer & Extended Programs, Box 1391, Portland, Oregon 97207; 503/725-8500 or 800/547-8887. Summer.

Oregon Association of Christian Writers Coaching Conference (in Salem), 17768 SW Pointe Forest Court, Aloha, Oregon 97006; 503/297-2987. August.

Oregon Association of Christian Writers Seminar (various locations), 17768 SW Pointe Forest Court, Aloha, Oregon 97006; 503/297-2987. Various.

OryCon, Box 5703, Portland, Oregon 97228. November.

SCBWI/NW Oregon Retreat (in Silver Falls, Oregon), 22736 Vanowen Street, Suite 106, West Hills, California 91307; 818/888-8760. Summer.

Summer Women's Writing Workshop (at Mckenzie Bridge), Flight of the Mind Workshops, 622 SE 29, Portland, Oregon 97214; 503/236-9862. July.

Willamette Writers Conference, 9045 SW Barbur Boulevard, Portland, Oregon 97219; 503/452-1592. August.

The Write Magic, 1140 Waverly Street, Eugene, Oregon 97401-5235; 503/485-0583. May.

PENNSYLVANIA

ConFluence, Box 3681, Pittsburgh, Pennsylvania 15230. July.

Cumberland Valley Fiction Writers' Workshop, Department of English, Dickinson College, Box 1773, Carlisle, Pennsylvania 17013-2896; 717/245-1291. June.

Dog Writers' Association of America (sites vary), Box E, Hummelstown, Pennsylvania 17036; 717/566-9843. February.

Highlights Foundation Writers Workshop at Chautauqua, Department NM, 711 Court Street, Honesdale, Pennsylvania 18431; 717/243-1192. July.

Ligonier Valley Writers Conference, RR4, Box 8, Ligonier, Pennsylvania 15658; 412/238-6397. July.

Mid-Atlantic Mystery Book Fair & Convention, Detecto Mysterioso Books at Society Hill Playhouse, 507 South 8th Street, Philadelphia, Pennsylvania 19147. November.

Outdoor Writers Association of America (sites vary), 2017 Cato Avenue, Suite 101, State College, Pennsylvania 16801-2768; 814/234-1011. June.

PennWriters Conference, RR2, Box 241, Middlebury Center, Pennsylvania 16935. May.

Philadelphia Writers' Conference, Box 7171, Philadelphia, Pennsylvania 19117; 215/782-1059. Various.

Philcon, Box 8303, 30th Street Station, Philadelphia, Pennsylvania 19101; 215/957-4004. November.

St. David's Christian Writers' Conference (in St. David), 1775 Eden Road, Lancaster, Pennsylvania 17601-3523; 717/394-6758. June.

Shooting Star Writers Conference, 7123 Race Street, Pittsburgh, Pennsylvania 15208-1424; 412/731-7464. October.

Young Writers at Penn Conference, Suite 100, 3440 Market Street, Philadelphia, Pennsylvania 19140-3335; 215/898-6763. March.

RHODE ISLAND

Necon, Box 528, East Greenwich, Rhode Island 02818. July.

Newport Writers Conference, Box 12, Newport, Rhode Island 02840; 401/846-9884. October.

SOUTH CAROLINA

The Charleston Writers' Conference, Lightsey Conference Center, College of Charleston, Charleston, South Carolina 29424; 803/953-8522. March.

Francis Marion Writers' Conference, Francis Marion University, Florence, South Carolina 29501; 803/661-1500. June.

Magnum Opus Con, Box 6585, Athens, Georgia 30604; 706/549-1533. March.

TENNESSEE

Chattanooga Conference on Southern Literature, Arts & Education Council, 424 Georgia Avenue, Chattanooga, Tennessee 37403; 615/267-1218. April.

Communicators Workshop: Writing for Publication, Desktop Publishing, Fund Development, Video Production, Box 370 Collegedale, Tennessee 37315; 800/768-8437 or 615/238-2730. May.

ConCat, 805 College Street, Knoxville, Tennessee 37921; 615/522-3470. November.

Concave, Box 3221, Kingsport, Tennessee 37664; 615/239-3106. February.

MidSouthCon, Box 22749, Memphis, Tennessee 38122; 901/274-7355. March.

Southern Baptist Writers' Workshop, 127 Ninth Avenue N., Nashville, Tennessee 37234; 615/251-2294. July.

A Touch of Success Writing Workshop for Photographers (in the Great Smoky Mountains), Box 194, Lowell, Florida 32663; 904/867-0463 or 502/769-1823. October.

TEXAS

Agents' Weekend Seminar, Suite E-2, 1501 W. 5th Street, Austin, Texas 78703. June.

AggieCon, MSC Cephid Variable, Box J-1, Memorial Student Center, College Station, Texas 77844; 409/845-1515. March.

AmigoCon, Box 3177, El Paso, Texas 79923; 915/542-0443. April.

Annual Writers Conference, NE Texas Community College, Continuing Education, Box 1307, Mt. Pleasant, Texas 75455; 903/272-1911. Spring.

ArmadilloCon, Box 9612, Austin, Texas 78766-9612; 512/266-9719. November.

Austin Writers' League Fall/Spring Workshops, E-2, 1501 W. Fifth, Austin, Texas 78703; 512/499-8914. Various.

Bride of Con-Troll, Box 740969-1025, Houston, Texas 77274; 713-895-9202. April.

Celebration of the Written Word, Southern Methodist University Literary Festival, SMU Box 436, Dallas, Texas 75275-0436; 214/768-4466. November.

Chisholm Trail Western Seminar, Texas Christian University, Box 32927, TCU Office of Extended Education, Ft. Worth, Texas 76129; 817/921-7134 or 800/TCU-7134. April.

ConTex, Box 541822, Houston, Texas 77254. November.

Craft of Writing, UTD Box 830688, CN 1.1, Richardson, Texas 75083; 214/690-2204. September.

Craft of Writing Conference, Center for Continuing Education, University of Texas/Dallas, Box 830688, Richardson, Texas 75083-0688; 214/690-2207. September.

Ft. Concho Museum Press Literary Festival, 213 East Avenue D, San Angelo, Texas 76903; 915/657-4441. August.

Golden Triangle Writers Guild, 4245 Calder, Beaumont, Texas 77705; 409/898-4894. October.

Hands-On Writer's Workshop, Box 1380, Lindale, Texas 75771; 903/883-9172 x.288. Various.

MacabreCon, Weasel Productions, Box 833105, Richardson, Texas 75083. November.

Panhandle-Plains Writers' Workshop, Wayland Baptist University, 1900 W. Seventh Street, Plainview, Texas 79072; 806/296-5521. July.

Rice University Publishing Program, School for Continuing Studies, Rice University, Box 1892, Houston, Texas 77251-1892; 713/527-4803. July–August.

Rice University Writers' Conference, School for Continuing Studies, Rice University, Box 1892, Houston, Texas 77251-1892; 713/527-4803. June.

Romance Writers of America National Conference (sites vary), Suite 315, 13700 Veteran Memorial Drive, Houston, Texas 77014; 713/440-6885. July.

Science Fiction Research Association (sites vary), 6021 Grassmere, Corpus Christi, Texas 78415; 512/855-9304. June.

Texas Outdoor Writers Association (in Brownwood), 1415 Northridge Drive, Austin, Texas 78723; 512/389-4570. January.

Texas Ranch Experience—Past & Present (in Richmond), Houston Council of Writers, Box 441381, Houston, Texas 77244-1381. September.

Write Move (in Mt. Pleasant, Texas), Box 260E, Route 6, Pittsburg, Texas 75686. April.

Write Way to Success Writers' Conference, Box 720661, Houston, Texas 77272-0661. April.

UTAH

Creative Writing Conference, Southern Utah University, Cedar City, Utah 84720; 801/586-1994. July.

Life, the Universe & Everything, 3163 JKHB, Provo, Utah 84602. February.

Writers at Work Conference, Box 1146, Centerville, Utah 84014-5146. June.

Writing Retreat/Canoe Trip with Sharon Olds (in Green River, Utah), Box 9109, Santa Fe, New Mexico 87504; 505/690-4490. October.

VERMONT

Bennington College Summer Writing Workshops, Bennington, Vermont 05201; 802/442-5401, x.320. July.

Bread Loaf Writers' Conference, Middlebury College, Middlebury, Vermont 05752; 802/388-3711, x.5286. August.

Dorothy Canfield Fisher Writers Conference (in Burlington), Box 1058, Waitsfield, Vermont 05673-1058; 802/496-3271. June.

League of Vermont Writers (in Burlington), Box 1058, Waitsfield, Vermont 05673; 802/496-3271. June.

The Olders' Travel Writing Workshops, Box 163, Albany, Vermont 05820; 802/755-6774. Various.

Vermont Studio Center Writing Studio Sessions, Box 613, Johnson, Vermont; 802/635-2727. Various.

Wildbranch Workshop in Outdoor, Natural History & Environmental Writing, Sterling College, Craftsbury Common, Vermont 05827; 800/648-3591. June.

Writers' Program at the Vermont Studio Center, Box 613P, Johnson, Vermont 05656; 802/635-2727. April.

VIRGINIA

Appalachian Writers Conference, Box 6935, Radford University, Radford, Virginia 24142-6935; 703/831-5269 or 703/639-0812. July.

Blue Ridge Writers Conference, 1942 Avon Road, Roanoke, Virginia 24015. October.

Christopher Newport University Writers' Conference, 50 Shoe Lane, Newport News, Virginia 23606; 804/594-7158. April.

Garden Writers Association of America (sites vary), 10210 Leatherleaf Court, Manassas, Virginia 22111; 703/257-1032. August.

Highland Summer Conference, Box 6935, Radford University, Radford, Virginia 24142; 703/831-5366. June.

Mythcon, 5465 N. Morgan Street, #106, Alexandria, Virginia 22312. August.

National Association of Black Journalists (sites vary), 11600 Sunrise Valley Drive, Reston, Virginia 22091; 703/648-1270. July.

National League of American Pen Women Conference (sites vary), Box 1707, Midlothian, Virginia 23112; 804/744-6503. Various.

Rising Star, 545 Howard Drive, Salem, Virginia 24153; 703/389-9400. October.

SCBWI/Mid-Atlantic, Box 1707, Midlothian, Virginia 23112; 804/744-6503. Fall.

Sci-Con, Box 9434, Hampton, Virginia 23670. November.

Selu Writers' Retreat, Box 6935, Radford University, Radford, Virginia 24142-6935; 703/831-5269. July.

Shenandoah Playwrights Retreat, Route 5, Box 1647F, Staunton, Virginia 24401; 703/248-1868. July–August.

Shenandoah Valley Writers Guild, Box 47, Middletown, Virginia 22645; 703/869-1120. May, November.

Society for Technical Communication's Conference (sites vary), Suite 904, 901 N. Stuart Street, Arlington, Virginia 22203-4114; 703/522-4114. May.

Technicon, Box 256, Blacksburg, Virginia 24063; 703/552-0572. April.

Women in Communications National Conference and Communicators Expo (sites vary), 2101 Wilson Boulevard, Suite 417, Arlington, Virginia 22201; 703/528-4200. October.

WASHINGTON

Clarion West Fiction & Science Fiction Writers' Workshop, Suite 350, 340 15th Avenue East, Seattle, Washington 98112; 206/322-9083. Summer.

ConComCom, Box 283, Seattle, Washington 98111. May.

Dreamcon, 10121 Evergreen Way, #1103, Everett, Washington 98204; 206/283-8090. October.

Incon, Box 1026, Spokane, Washington 99201. October.

Neurocon, 24026 21st Avenue S., Seattle, Washington 98198; 206/365-1740. February.

Norwescon, NWSFS, Box 24207, Seattle, Washington 98124; 206/248-2010. March.

Pacific NW Writers Summer Conference, 2033 6th Avenue, #804, Seattle, Washington 98121; 206/443-3807. July.

Port Townsend Writer's Conference, Centrum Foundation, Box 1158, Port Townsend, Washington 98368; 206/385-3102 or 800/733-3608. July.

Potlach, Box 31848, Seattle, Washington 98103. February.

Rustycon, Box 84201, Seattle, Washington 98124-5591. January.

San Juan Islands Writers' Retreat (on Whidbey Island), 1200 Midland Building, Des Moines, Iowa 50309; 800/551-9453. October.

Seattle Pacific University Christian Writers' Institute, Humanities Department, Seattle, Washington 98119; 206/281-2109. June.

Write on the Sound Writers' Conference, 700 Main Street, Edmonds, Washington 98020; 206/771-0228. October.

Writers' Weekend at the Beach, Box 877, Ocean Park, Washington 98640; 206/665-6576. February.

WEST VIRGINIA

The Blue Ridge Mountains Writers' Retreat (at Berkeley Springs, West Virginia), 1200 Midland Building, Des Moines, Iowa 50309; 800/551-9453. November.

GoldenRod Writers' Conference, 219 Kingwood Street, Morgantown, West Virginia 26505; 304/296-9132. October.

West Virginia Authors Weekend, 219 Kingwood Street, Morgantown, West Virginia 26505; 304/296-9132. September.

WISCONSIN

Best Writers' Workshop in the World, Redbird Studios, 3195 S. Superior, Milwaukee, Wisconsin 53207; 414/481-3029. April.

A Day with an Editor (in Stevens Point), Box 736, Thiensville, Wisconsin 53092; 414/242-9548. September.

Great Lakes Writer's Workshop, Alverno College, 3401 S. 39 Street, Box 343922, Milwaukee, Wisconsin 53234-3922; 414/382-6176. July.

Green Lake Christian Writers Conference, American Baptist Assembly, Highway 23, Green Lake, Wisconsin 54951-9589; 800/558-8898. July.

Ocooch Mountain Writers' Retreat, 1200 Highway 14 W., Richland Center, Wisconsin 53581; 608/647-6186. July.

SCBWI/Wisconsin Retreat, 26 Lancaster Court, Madison, Wisconsin 53719-1433; 608/271-0433. Fall.

School of the Arts at Rhinelander (in Rhinelander), University of Wisconsin/Madison, 726 Lowell Hall, 610 Langdon Street, Madison, Wisconsin 53703. July.

WisCon, Box 1624, Madison, Wisconsin 53701-1624; 608/233-8850. March.

Wisconsin Regional Writer's Association Spring Conference, Barefoot Bay Lodge, Elkhart Lake, Wisconsin; 414/565-2592. May.

The Write Touch, Box 92277, Milwaukee, Wisconsin 53202. May.

WYOMING

American Literature and the Spirit of Place (in Jackson Hole), Box 128, Wilson, Wyoming 83014; 307/733-2214. August.

Jackson Hole Writers' Conference (in Jackson Hole), Box 3972, University of Wyoming Conferences & Institutes, Laramie, Wyoming 82071-3972; 800/448-7801 or 307/766-2124. July.

The Teacher as Writer (in Jackson Hole), Box 128, Wilson, Wyoming 83014; 307/733-2214. August.

Your Journal Brought to Life (in Jackson Hole), Box 128, Wilson, Wyoming 83014; 307/733-2214. June.

CANADA

Association pour l'Avancement des Sciences et des Techniques de la Documentation (in Sherbrooke, Quebec), 1030 rue Cherrier, Suite 505, Montreal, Quebec H2L 1H9 CANADA; 514/52ASTED. October.

Can*Con, Box 5752, Merivale Depot, Nepeau, Ontario K2C 3M1 CANADA. May.

Canadian Authors Association Conference (in Waterloo), Suite 500, 275 Slater Street, Ottawa, Ontario K1P 5H9 CANADA; 613/233-2846. June.

International PEN World Congress (sites vary), The Writers Centre, 24 Ryerson Avenue, Toronto, Ontario M5T 2P3 CANADA; 416/860-1448. Fall.

Maritime Writers' Workshop, University of New Brunswick, Box 4400, Fredericton, New Brunswick E3B 5A3 CANADA; 506/453-4646. July.

Periodical Writers' Association of Canada (sites vary), Writer's Center, 24 Ryerson Avenue, Toronto, Ontario M5T 2P3 CANADA; 416/868-6913. June.

RhinoCon, Box 151, Alisa Craig, Ontario, N0M 1A0 Canada. March.

Summer Writers' Workshop, Writing from the Edge (at Atlin Wilderness Centre), Box 207, Atlin, British Columbia V0W 1A0 CANADA; 416/536-7971. August.

INTERNATIONAL

Australian National Science Fiction & Media Con, Box 212, World Trade Centre, Melbourne VIC 3005, Australia. April.

Beneluxcon/Con-Yak, James Wattstraat 13, 1097 DJ Amsterdam, The Netherlands; 31-20-6934346. November.

EuroCon, ARSFan, Street Paris nr 1, 1900 Timisoara, Romania. May.

Frankfurt Book Fair, Box 10 01 16, Reineckstrasse 3, 6000 Frankfurt am Main 1, Germany. October.

InteriorCon, 109/163 - bl 2, Sao Paolo-SP, CEP 01252-901 Brazil. November.

International Readers Theatre Workshop (in London), Institute for Readers Theatre, Box 17193, San Diego, California 92177; 619/276-1948. July.

Making Waves with Writers (on a Caribbean cruise aboard the SS *Norway*), NAU Box 5638, Flagstaff, Arizona 86011; 602/523-3559. June.

Mexico Fiction Workshops (in Acapulco), 3584 Kirkwood Place, Boulder, Colorado 80304; 303/444-0086. February.

New Zealand National Con, Box 333, Dunedin, New Zealand. June.

Nordcon, Gdanski Klub Fantastikyi, Box 76, Gdansk 37 80-325, Poland; 48-58-531-073. December.

Novacon, 121 Cape Hill, Smethwick, Warley, West Midlands, UK B66 4SH; 021-558-0997. November.

OctoCon/Ireland, 20 Newgrove Avenue, Sandymount, Dublin 4, Ireland. October.

Paris-American Academy Writing Workshop (in Paris), Box 102, HC 01, Plainview, Texas 79072; 806/889-3533. July.

Writing for Children, Union Hall, Skibbereen, County Cork, Ireland; 011-353-28-22407. June, July.

Writing Retreat/Canoe Trip with Deena Metzger (in Baja, Mexico), Box 9109, Santa Fe, New Mexico 87504; 505/690-4490. November.

One Final Note: For WesterCon, WorldCon, World Fantasy Con, World Horror Con, BoucherCon, and the like, since the contact information changes from one year to the next, your fastest bet is to check recent issues of *Locus* (see the Bibliography). Good hunting!

Bibliography

MAGAZINES

Locus, Locus Publications, PO Box 13305, Oakland, California 94661; 510/339-9196. Monthly.

Poets & Writers Magazine, 72 Spring Street, New York, New York 10012; 212/226-3586. Bimonthly.

Premiere, Box 7079, Red Oak, Iowa 51566-0079; 800/289-2489. Monthly.

Publishers Weekly, Box 1979, Marion, Ohio 42206-2079; 800/842-1669. Weekly.

The Writer, 120 Boylston Street, Boston, Massachusetts 02116. Monthly.

Writer's Digest, Box 2124, Harlan, Iowa 51593-2313. Monthly.

WRITER'S Journal, Minnesota Ink, Inc., 3585 N Lexington Avenue, Suite 328, Arden Hills, Minnesota 55126-8056. Bimonthly.

MARKET LISTINGS

Literary Market Place, RR Bowker, 121 Chanlon Road, New Providence, New Jersey 07974-1541; 908/464-6800. Updated annually.

Children's Writer's & Illustrator's Market
Guide to Literary Agents and Art/Photo Reps
Market Guide for Young Writers (updated periodically)
Mystery Writer's Market Place and Sourcebook (updated periodically)
Novel & Short Story Writer's Market
Poet's Market
Photographer's Market
Songwriter's Market
Writer's Market

> All available from Writer's Digest Books, 1507 Dana Avenue, Cincinnati, Ohio 45207; 800/289-0963. Updated annually, unless otherwise specified.

About the Authors

Steven D. Spratt and **Lee G. Spratt** have been partners, writers, editors, and teachers since 1985, and, amazingly, are still married. While they almost never argue in their married life, they freely admit having stood forehead-to-forehead, screaming at each other, over the placement of a comma. Ah, the joys of collaboration!

Before picking up the pen (or, in their case, the keyboard), Steve was a laborer, logger, reluctant soldier, and corporate climber. He grew up all over the northwestern United States before finally settling down in Portland, Oregon, in 1983. Lee is a Portland native who spent a dozen years as a legal secretary before succumbing to the writing bug.

Their publishing credits include *Scars*, a short story collection (Strawberry Hill Press, 1993); *Showdown*, a western paperback novella (DimeNovels!, 1991); and over eighty short stories—so far. Their fiction interests range from westerns to horror to the science fiction/technothriller they're currently completing. They've also taught writing marketable fiction since 1991, and are as hooked on teaching as they are on writing.